RIGHT BRAIN / LEFT BRAIN LEADERSHIP

RIGHT BRAIN / LEFT BRAIN LEADERSHIP

Shifting Style for Maximum Impact

Mary Lou Décosterd

Foreword by Jerri L. Frantzve

Contemporary Psychology
Chris E. Stout, Series Editor

Westport, Connecticut
London

Library of Congress Cataloging-in-Publication Data

Décosterd, Mary Lou.
  Right brain/left brain leadership : shifting style for maximum impact /
  Mary Lou Décosterd ; foreword by Jerri L. Frantzve.
    p. cm. — (Contemporary psychology, ISSN 1546–668X)
  Includes bibliographical references and index.
  ISBN 978–0–275–99934–6 (alk. paper)
  1. Leadership. 2. Left and right (Psychology) 3. Laterality. 4. Cerebral
dominance. I. Title.
  BF637.L4D43 2008
  658.4'092—dc22   2008004552

British Library Cataloguing in Publication Data is available.

Library of Congress Catalog Card Number: 2008004552
ISBN: 978–0–275–99934–6
ISSN: 1546–668X

First published in 2008

Praeger Publishers, 88 Post Road West, Westport, CT 06881
An imprint of Greenwood Publishing Group, Inc.
www.praeger.com

Printed in the United States of America

The paper used in this book complies with the
Permanent Paper Standard issued by the National
Information Standards Organization (Z39.48–1984).

10 9 8 7 6 5 4 3 2 1

Copyright Acknowledgments

The book contains case examples. All case examples are fictitious. Public figures referred to in this book were not interviewed. Descriptions of public figures are based on publicly available information.

The book contains information about health and fitness. Readers should not regard any and all such information as a substitute for medical advice or prescription. The author and publisher disclaim responsibility for any adverse effects arising from the application of any health and fitness information contained in this book.

To my husband, Jean-Pierre, a model business leader, to Jerri, my alter-brain mentor, and to my mom, Rosemarie, my personal inspiration.

CONTENTS

ILLUSTRATIONS

SERIES FOREWORD

What a pleasure it was to read Mary Lou's work. I was taken back to the morning we first spoke of the concept. I was driving to a meeting, and though I was (as usual) running late, I sat in the parking lot at my destination as I was so captivated by her notion for this model as well as this book.

The bookstore shelves are filled with leadership wannabe guides and volumes on the unexpected movements of cheese and sixty-second-this, four-hour-that and seven steps to most everything. In my humble opinion, those are the rants of quick fix gurus looking to up-sell readers into subscribing to their workshops and whatnots or the howls of dinosaurs.

It is thus so refreshing to read *Right Brain / Left Brain Leadership*. Mary Lou is on to something—something born of the science of understanding the biological hardwiring we all possess, but with application in the very real world of applied leadership. Mary Lou steps well beyond the not-so-helpful dichotomy of the nature/nurture aspects of leadership to a synthetic model of how one cognitively ticks—the strengths and the weaknesses—to real-world application.

I particularly enjoyed the format she uses in conveying her concepts; she has taken complex aspects and made them accessible to all readers but without any dumbing down. Readers are provided with actionable tools, not tired dictums or repackaged common sense. *Right Brain / Left Brain Leadership* is destined to become a primary tool for those destined

to become better leaders. My tip of the hat to Mary Lou; she has done
what so many have tried.

Chris E. Stout, PsyD, MBA

Kildeer, Illinois

January 2008

FOREWORD

Picture a vice president of manufacturing drawing with crayons to capture his vision for the future of his organization. Not a usual tool for leadership development, is it? Or, see a marketing executive posting a spider in a web on her computer as a cue to remind her to build relationships across functions within her division. These are just a few of the techniques Dr. Mary Lou Décosterd recommends, and uses, to encourage leaders to extend themselves beyond their preferences, to shift style in order to lead from their right and left brain—not as an exception, but as a rule.

Dr. Décosterd's expertise in human behavior, the brain, and learning applied to a leader's personal best is a refreshing and powerful combination. Stressing the psychological aspects of leading through ten guiding behaviors, along with using innovative tools and in-the-moment rejuvenators to help access these behaviors, has, in the almost fifteen years we have worked together, netted us dramatic results. More importantly, Dr. Décosterd has successfully moved countless leaders to try actions out of their zones of comfort in order to expand the breadth and depth of their abilities.

Right Brain/Left Brain Leadership: Shifting Style for Maximum Impact successfully integrates current thoughts on leadership, the role of brain functioning in behavior and creativity, and wellness tools for expanding leadership potential, and it ties all this together with a comprehensive roadmap for individual success.

By pulling together a wealth of very diverse material into a complex, holistic model of leadership for the current times, Dr. Décosterd offers something new, different, and valuable to the leadership field. By writing for the practitioner, she offers an effective approach to personal and professional development—one that is built on solid science and practice. By including notes and references to relevant subject matter experts (SMEs) in the leadership, health, and science fields, she offers depth and models a process for organizing and integrating leadership knowledge.

So, what can you expect? A lot! While weaving science, theory, and practice together in a manner that models what she is teaching, Dr. Décosterd offers a whole that is much more than the sum of its parts.

The chapter on brain functioning offers a review of relevant research that links how our brains operate to leadership, without breaking into such scientific jargon and detail that it makes one glassy-eyed. Assuming that most of you are like me—not well versed in this area—I think you will find it comprehensive, yet understandable in its explanations, examples, and implications for your leadership development. This is refreshing! During the American Psychological Association's declared "Decade of the Brain," I attended a colleague's symposium on his innovative approach to cognitive functioning. The model was brilliant; however, I understood less than ten percent of its application. Dr. Décosterd distills the essence of the past several decades of research regarding the functioning of the brain into clear reasoning and application. Thank you!

Dr. Décosterd's model is presented in a chaining approach that builds each successive step on our understanding of the previous one. She introduces terms and approaches in a manner that mirrors her application of integration as key to success. You will find yourself reminded to consistently move beyond preferences to maximize your impact. This is certainly not a cookie-cutter, one-size-fits-all approach. With the ten guiding leadership behaviors broken down into 100 traits, tailoring is afforded to individual strengths and weaknesses—which we all have!

I admired Mary Lou before I read this book. I've been an active observer—though not always a quiet one—as she has developed her work and this model over our many years of working together. That said, I know firsthand that if you work with the material she presents in this book, you will have greater impact on your organization—as a more effective leader!

Jerri L. Frantzve, PhD
Placitas, New Mexico
November 2007

Chapter 1

Leadership, Life, and the Brain

Only that which is the other gives us truly unto ourselves.

—*Sri Yogananda*

Shifting Style for Maximum Impact

What is it that we need from leaders today? What would make a leader truly great? How can our leaders help us experience all that is at our disposal while getting us through the challenges we face? In other words, different from at other times in history, what does it take to be a leader today? And most importantly, how can I become a better leader, one who can measure up to the expectations of our times? These are the questions this book will address.

Never before has life been so exciting, so rich with opportunity—and never before have our challenges been so complex. Pick up a newspaper, surf the internet, turn on a television, or go to work, and on any given day you will be struck by both what we have at our disposal and what we struggle with. In all that we do, we look to our leaders for guidance, support, and resolution. Given the changes in society, leaders today are signing up for a new set of responsibilities. A new perspective on leadership is needed to assist them.

As an executive consultant working with leaders from a wide mix of businesses and organizations, from chief executive officers (CEOs) of large profit companies to principals of local schools, I see clearly that the most successful leaders are the ones who have the greatest breadth and flexibility in style and perspective. Leaders today need to be intuitive and compelling, able to see the way and rally their people while always anticipating obstacles. They must be able to sift through massive demands and drive focus. They must communicate information and context with clarity, keeping everyone and everything on track. They must motivate, inspire, and empower in the face of what seems, to most, insurmountable obstacles. This is what is expected of leaders today. As a leader, can you meet these expectations? Is it reasonable to assume that any one person can act with such leadership breadth?

Some of us are compelling, others are intuitive, and still others are great at seeing a process through from beginning to end. Some leaders are better at leading people and others at driving for results. Most leaders are strong in purpose, capability, and conviction but have, over the years, developed certain styles and approaches that work well for them in some situations while constricting their impact in others. And when leaders are challenged, they tend to do more of what they are the most comfortable doing, rather than looking for a different way.

This is not new information, that all of us, leaders included, have certain behavioral preferences we have developed over the years. If you have taken part in professional development experiences, you know that such experiences teach us to better understand and leverage our existing style. They also teach us to modify our style to accommodate those with differing approaches. At times they may even show us how to extend beyond our preferences.

I challenge leaders to go a step farther, to extend beyond your preferences, not as an exception but as a rule. To have what it takes to lead in today's world you will need to broaden your skill sets by continually adding new or different actions to your repertoire—I refer to these new actions as alter-brain behaviors.

An alter-brain behavior is a style shift resulting in a new action that, when accessed, can give either greater depth to a preferred style or complementary breadth to your overall approach.

While we tend to act from constricted preferences, our brains are set up for much more: our brains are set up for greater breadth and depth. You may have heard it said that we use only a small part of our brains. For most of us, this is certainly true. Expressions like "we are creatures of habit" and "great minds think alike" illustrate our tendencies toward what is known and familiar. The expression "opposites attract" refers to an emotional pull, an excitement we feel when we are in the company of someone or something different. All too often, though, our excitement turns sour. While we gravitate toward the different, we are socialized to what we already know. We sometimes say that we don't like to "step out of our comfort zones," another indicator of how we unwittingly thwart our brain's diverse potential. By focusing on alter-brain behaviors, our brain's own natural power can be renewed.

In the coming chapters you will learn to shift style in order to access and leverage a wide range of leadership behaviors. You will be given techniques and processes to enhance how you interact with others and drive for results. You will be introduced to a new leadership model, one that will enable you to function with maximum leadership impact.

Leadership Today

Since this is a book about leadership, perhaps we should start by defining some basic terms. A leader is defined as "a person or thing that leads, a guiding or directing head, the principal player in an organization." Leadership is defined as "the position or function of a leader, the ability to lead."[1] If we were to look at leadership in the broadest sense, we could say that leadership is acting from a specific position and/or acumen in order to impact situations and make a difference.[2]

Think for a moment of the leaders you have known. Think about individuals who have led you. Think also about who you are as a leader. If you were asked what makes a leader great, what would you say? Here is what I was told when I asked my clients that question:

Great leaders know what they are doing and let others do their job.

A great leader has a vision that we all know and understand.

A great leader makes me want to push myself and is someone I look up to.

Great leaders inspire me and while they aren't afraid to take risks, they aren't reckless either.

A great leader tells us what we need to know.

A great leader has great ways of conceptualizing things.

A great leader makes good decisions—ones we can live with.

Great leaders hold us accountable; they are tough, but fair.

The really great leaders know how to handle themselves.

A great leader is someone who considers all possibilities and helps us make the changes we need to make.

Diversity Among Leaders

As you read over these comments about leaders, you should have seen yourself in some of them. Each of us who leads has certain hallmarks. Over the years and through our many assignments and experiences, we have honed certain values, processes, and actions that net us success. What is interesting is the variation from one successful leader to another. If you were to examine ten leadership accomplishments, you would see ten very different success measures.

Look at the following well-known leaders: Martin Luther King Jr., Rudy Giuliani, Golda Meir, Herb Brooks, Jack Welch, and Oprah Winfrey. Martin Luther King directed our civil rights movement. Rudy Giuliani led the response to an unprecedented national crisis. Golda Meir became prime minister of Israel following a lifelong career of service to her country. Coach Brooks led the 1980 underdog U.S. Olympic hockey team to its gold medal. Jack Welch led the largest corporate turnaround in recent history. Oprah Winfrey created an empire as one the most influential voices on contemporary social issues. Each of these leaders achieved greatness, and each is as different from the other as are their contributions.

Martin Luther King was inspirational in both voice and action. His conviction, passion, and genuineness made us want to listen and follow him. Giuliani's visibility and presence, his felt leadership following the events of September 11, 2001 provided his city and the nation with a sense of grounding at a time of great shock and pain. Golda Meir was revered for her total dedication to her people. She was as independent as she was connected and as tough as she was caring. Herb Brooks led with conviction and perseverance from an organized, methodical plan and pushed a team beyond what they and the world thought possible. Jack Welch created a new operating culture in the face of fierce opposition and drove adherence to that new culture with tenacity, alignment, and consistency. Oprah Winfrey's keen insight, relentless candor, and engaging style enable her to continue to raise full-spectrum life issues in a way that is accessible to the masses.

It is interesting to envision what would happen if these leaders were to switch places. How would Jack Welch do in Israel? Could "Rudy" host an "Oprah" show? What would Golda Meir have said to the hockey team at the end of the second period? How would Martin Luther King have fared during 9/11? Could Herb Brooks have led a civil rights rally? What would General Electric's results have looked like in Jack's era with Oprah at the helm? Chances are, some of what made each of these leaders great in one situation would translate well to a different circumstance, while some of their strengths and styles would not play so well.

Even though these six leaders are high-profile individuals, what was expected of each of them is not far from what most leaders will encounter at one time or another in their careers. We will all be expected to be inspirational, to lead in critical times, to push our people beyond the norm, to accomplish the greater good, to drive execution and accountability, and to raise issues. As such, leaders today can no longer be comfortable with a style or range of impact that makes them better in one situation than another. Leaders must prepare for and expect of themselves broader impact skills.

Diversity Within Leaders

With that in mind, following are described ten behaviors that equate to broad leadership impact. These ten behaviors cut across contexts and styles and to one degree or another will be needed by leaders in the near and long term and in the handling of special events. Take a moment to rate yourself on each behavior. The rating scale goes from zero (0) to ten (10) with zero being no ability whatsoever and ten being stellar, no room for improvement. When rating yourself, consider your broad impact. Think of how you interact among groups—up, down, and across the organization. Your ratings for each behavior should take into account all possibilities of what is expected of you and represent an average of your ability.

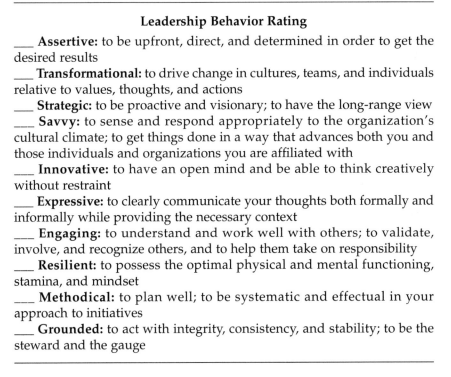

Leadership Behavior Rating

___ **Assertive:** to be upfront, direct, and determined in order to get the desired results

___ **Transformational:** to drive change in cultures, teams, and individuals relative to values, thoughts, and actions

___ **Strategic:** to be proactive and visionary; to have the long-range view

___ **Savvy:** to sense and respond appropriately to the organization's cultural climate; to get things done in a way that advances both you and those individuals and organizations you are affiliated with

___ **Innovative:** to have an open mind and be able to think creatively without restraint

___ **Expressive:** to clearly communicate your thoughts both formally and informally while providing the necessary context

___ **Engaging:** to understand and work well with others; to validate, involve, and recognize others, and to help them take on responsibility

___ **Resilient:** to possess the optimal physical and mental functioning, stamina, and mindset

___ **Methodical:** to plan well; to be systematic and effectual in your approach to initiatives

___ **Grounded:** to act with integrity, consistency, and stability; to be the steward and the gauge

This brief self-assessment will begin to give you a sense of your leadership depth and breadth. High scores on a specific behavior (a score of 7 or better) point to a possible depth strength. A high breadth score would be a score of 7 or better for seven or more individual behaviors. Your goal should be to get and keep yourself at a high breadth score. Do you think you can do it? Look over the ten behaviors again. Some of the behaviors are similar or complementary, while others are opposites. Is it reasonable for a leader to develop opposing preferences? Can we be of two minds? Being of two minds is precisely what alter-brain behaviors are all about. When engaging an alter-brain behavior you move from a preferred behavior, your typical way of acting, to a different action. You shift your style for maximum impact.

Consider the following scenario: You are a leader with a high score in the behavior assertive. You are at work, going through your usual motions, driving hard to get things done. You come back to your office, look over your tracking data, and see that two teams are behind schedule on their projects. You dig a bit deeper and find that the new processes that were put in place are not being followed. Your inclination is to confront the situation. You get prepared to push everyone back on track. You've been here before and know that if you make it clear that you are not going to back down, everything will fall into place. The problem today, though, is that your people are not resisting or slacking off; they are stuck. A few of them think that the path they are heading down is going to create problems in the long run, but they don't really know why. They just sense it. They know that in order to get you to listen, they need to come to you with more than a feeling. So, they are keeping quiet for now.

What could you do? You could keep pushing (high assertive response). You could call a meeting with the key players to discuss the problem (moderate, but still an assertive response). Both of these options are typical for someone with an assertive style for three reasons: they are forward in motion, they involve interaction with others, and they are focused on the existing reality, on "what is."

Alter-brain thinking would suggest something different, a shift, for example, to an innovative response. An innovative response is solitary (involves just you, at least initially) and is focused on what might be. For the next two hours you could access this alter-brain innovative behavior with a creative reflection. Here is what you could do. Get in your car and go somewhere off-site for lunch, somewhere quiet. Sit away from the crowd, clear your mind, and think. Don't think about what to do. Think about what is going on. Get out a piece of paper and a pen and on the top half of the paper draw the way things were when you left—some symbol to represent the mess. It's not about being an artist; it is about using the parts of your brain that are nonverbal, that are visual, just for a moment. Now on the bottom half of the paper draw how you want things to be—again, find your symbol or depiction—no words, just drawings. Think about the players and the circumstances. Think about the patterns surrounding the issue. Now it's time to write. Jot down your thoughts. What might be causing the problems? What could you do that is different from what you would normally do? You will return to the situation with different insights, new information, and perhaps a new action. The slight shift in your style will be noticeable to your team, and it will jog them to respond in kind with different behaviors as well. You have changed the dynamic, and you will get a different result.

Leadership Vulnerability

Expanding the behaviors from which you lead makes you more nimble. Not doing so leaves you vulnerable. Such vulnerability is aptly expressed by one senior vice president who relayed that never before had he worked harder, accomplished more, and felt less successful.

Today's leadership vulnerability is evidenced in a number of ways. Some leaders are reaching goals they never thought possible and are being asked yet for more. Other leaders are coming into broken situations confident they can turn things around but finding it more difficult than they thought. New leaders are given more and more responsibility with less and less experience or training and are becoming quickly overwhelmed. Still others feel ineffectual at addressing escalating people challenges, like low morale. Some simply cannot keep up with the rate and pace of change. The net result is that many of today's solid leaders are getting the message that they aren't making it. Bright, capable, hard-working, well-intentioned leaders are receiving lower performance ratings, being moved out of assignments, or are holding their own but never really feeling on top of things. The lucky ones are succeeding but at greater personal cost.

So what is happening? Simply put, the rules have changed. In the past, it was enough for a solid leader to leverage his or her strengths and for the most part succeed. Today however, with intensified profitability challenges, greater workforce complexities, new environmental and social circumstances, and the world moving at lightning speed, it is harder for leaders to get to the goal line. In order to succeed in today's work climate, leaders need to act from a broader, more complete range of business, organizational, and interpersonal behaviors.

Right Brain/Left Brain Leadership: Shifting Style for Maximum Impact was written to offer today's leaders a new model and process for broader leadership engagement. Through such broader engagement, leaders will increase their range and be more able to meet today's leadership demands.

Life: A Case Study Approach

Four cases will be introduced to bring this book to life: four leaders and their leadership situations. These cases are fictional representations of mainstream leaders and the challenges they face. Meet Angela, Ken, Madison, and Peter.

Angela

Angela is vice president of U.S. sales for a multinational company. She has a BA in business and an MBA. Angela has held two previous sales director positions for smaller organizations. She has been with her present company for two years. Most of the members of her sales force have been with the company much longer and have a set way of looking at the company and their work. She just received word from her boss that their stretch targets have been accelerated. Angela knows what that means. While her team has not only outperformed the other divisions but also increased their gross profitability from last year, their chances of hitting these new targets are slim to none. Bonuses are now at risk. Two key team members had seen this coming and left within two months of each other. Morale is noticeably down.

Angela is seen as a solid leader, someone others trust and who is accessible. She is good at formal and informal recognition and at involving and empowering her team. She is organized and logical, and she manages well across the organization. She is a good communicator and tries to approach her work with great enthusiasm. Confrontation is not her strong suit, however. She believes in trying to work around conflict rather than tackling it head on. The workload is getting to Angela, and she is showing signs of stress and fatigue.

The ever-escalating stretch targets pose two interrelated challenges for her. Given what the company is expecting in terms of numbers, Angela's team needs to increase sales and work differently within the greater organization. In particular, they need to be open to new ways of addressing marketplace challenges. While her people are loyal and willing to work hard, they are not open to changing how they view the business or how they approach their work. She will first need to confront their stagnant mindset and then help them reposition themselves in order to reach their goals.

Ken

Ken is the new CEO of a nonprofit organization. He is meeting with his executive team to begin to craft a five-year strategy for the board. While their business has historically been viewed as stable, they have not been without problems. Ken was brought in from the outside to address nagging cultural issues. He replaced three key members of the executive team as soon as he took over, which caused quite a commotion. He is still not sure he has the right team in place. What he is sure of is that he needs to grow the company's bottom line and develop its centers of excellence. To do so he must address the issues that are holding them back, in particular, matters related to customer service and quality.

Ken is a seasoned administrator having held leadership positions at prominent related organizations. He is seen as formidable, logical, focused, and pragmatic. He is a results-oriented driver and is able to take a long-range view. He talks a lot, perhaps too much at times. He has a high level of energy and is a fitness buff. Ken is active in his local community, believing strongly in giving back. Ken has a command and control style. He thinks and acts quickly and is more comfortable directing than discussing. He is viewed as lacking patience. Once he sets his mind on a course, his expectation is that others get on board.

Ken has to make changes to the culture of his organization and to the mindset of those who work there. His leadership presence will be critical to how he is able to fare. He can easily set the direction and detail the plan, but meeting the interpersonal demands of his charge will be more difficult for him.

Madison

Madison is a young executive who has just been promoted to director of a creative team responsible for several key initiatives. This is her first leadership assignment. Madison has a BA in commercial art. She was born in California and moved with her family to New York when she was in high school. Madison liked New York so much she decided to go to school in the city and begin her career there.

Madison's company is new and high profile. Their greatest challenge moving forward will be to keep pace with their customer demands and continue to grow their market position. While the company culture is one of high energy and enthusiasm, it is beginning to feel frenetic. Employees are barely covering workloads, and there is a pervasive reactive quality to the work. No one is quite clear about the direction moving forward. An additional strain is the growing staff turnover, as many are being wooed away by the competition.

Madison is one of the company's high-potential young leaders. She has good energy and ideas and is open and animated. She enjoys solid relationships within her team and across the organization. She is good at anticipating problems and contributing to problem-solving discussions. Like many young leaders, Madison often overlooks the subtle but powerful political undercurrents, and her influencing style is one of persuasion rather than direction. She has been criticized for lacking focus, and some were surprised that she was promoted so quickly. Her greatest challenge is to prioritize the work. She must also ensure that projects are well managed and that the work is resourced as effectively as possible while overseeing quality and communications to internal customers.

Peter

Peter has just been promoted from assistant plant manager of one facility to plant manager of another. Peter's plant is a newly acquired overseas facility. He was considered for this position, in part, because of his prior experiences living and working in the same region. It was felt that he would relate well to the staff and local community. Peter came to this company four years ago and has had two prior assignments with them. Peter is expected to integrate this new facility into the larger organization and to do so quickly. Peter must also build relationships with the plant's two primary customers in Asia.

Peter is a solid plant leader. His educational background is in engineering, and he knows the product and the production line well. In his initial meetings with his new staff he was pleased to find a solid team. With respect to his overall plant, Peter sees that he will have to make several people changes and he is comfortable doing so. Those who work for Peter see him as fair, capable, and stable. Peter is also well respected by his superiors, having been successful in his two previous assignments. Managing up and down are Peter's strengths. Peter is not, however, as adept with peers and colleagues. They see him as difficult to deal with.

The challenge for Peter in quickly and successfully integrating his plant into the greater organization will be twofold. First, he must work more collaboratively across the organization, building stronger business partnerships. The second challenge Peter faces is a cultural one. Peter will need to broaden his cultural expertise and use it toward establishing effective ongoing dialogue not just with a diverse peer group, but with his new customer groups, among whom he has not had much previous exposure.

Angela, Ken, Madison, and Peter face complex leadership challenges. They share some similar talents and are also unique in many respects. They are not unlike the rest of us. We all have much capability at our disposal—some we leverage; some we don't. Our capabilities come to us from the workings of our brain. Knowing more about how our brain works can help us more fully tap into our potentials.

The Brain: What Leaders Need to Know

As a leader, you function as an executive over an assigned scope of work. Those who report to you and work along with you are well served when they understand the ways in which you function. They need to see how you react and know your preferred processes to know how to best support you. Your brain functions as an executive over you. Your brain, like you, needs to be understood relative to its ways of functioning, how it reacts, and its preferred processes, so that you can best support it. Leaders need a working knowledge of the brain in order to best influence it and access its full power and potential.

Leaders benefit from knowledge of the brain for yet another reason. Your brain provides a model for how organizations and teams within organizations should function. Your brain is your perfect business model. Leaders can look to the brain to see systems and functions that work. The brain is a system of roles, specializations, and collaborations like no company or business I have yet come across. As you are reading about how your brain works and how behavior is generated, think of the implications for how your organization could run, how you would like to perform as a leader, and how you would like your team to perform. The brain is truly our most diversified and integrated business unit.

The information presented on the brain will focus on how the brain impacts behavior and will be organized into five segments. The first segment will look at structure and function—how your brain is physically organized and what each area of the brain does or controls. The second segment will look at stress and emotions, the third at how the brain interprets and modulates social response, and the fourth at the nature of social/emotional leadership ability. The final segment will provide you with an executive summary, your high-level need to know about your brain as it relates to leadership.

The Brain and Nervous System: Structure and Function

The forebrain is the largest and most complex structure in the human brain. It is divided into two hemispheres, the right and left (see Figure 1.1). The brain's hemispheres are separated by a groove called the longitudinal fissure. The hemispheres are connected primarily by a cluster of nerve fibers called the corpus callosum. The corpus callosum allows the two hemispheres of the brain to communicate with and integrate areas of functional specialization.[3]

Each hemisphere is additionally divided into lobes. While the two sets of lobes are physical mirror images of each other, each lobe specializes in controlling different aspects of our behavior. The frontal lobes enable us to plan, execute, and control impulses. The parietal lobes give us information about where we are in relation to objects around us, they allow us to know what something is by touching it, and they allow us to sense cold, warmth, and pain. The occipital lobes enable us to know what we are seeing by interpreting shape, color, and other qualities, while the temporal lobes are involved in hearing, understanding meaning, and visually identifying familiar objects, like someone's face.[4]

In the 1960s, Roger Sperry and his team of researchers discovered that the right and left hemispheres of the brain directed different aspects of our mental ability. Sperry's findings about the brain's hemispheres won

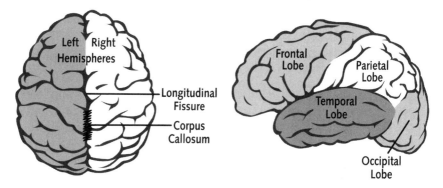

Figure 1.1 Divisions of the Forebrain

him the Nobel Prize in Medicine and changed the way we viewed both the mind and our behavior.

We Are of Two Minds

What we came to understand from the work of Sperry and, later, others was that the left hemisphere was instrumental in logical thought and reasoning, while the right hemisphere generated more unstructured thought. Specifically, the left side of the brain controls sequential and linear thought. It is where our verbal and analytical abilities come from. The left brain helps us to see things as they are. It is ordered, quantitative in orientation, logical, realistic, and practical. The left brain reasons from part to whole and communicates in names and labels. The right brain, on the other hand, controls intuitive and emotional thought. It is imaginative, nonverbal, and holistic. The right brain reasons from whole to parts, is reflective, and thinks of the world as it could be.[5] This knowledge of left and right brain abilities led to the descriptor that "we are of two minds."

Which of these characteristics or preferences do you see in yourself? Are you more left- or right-brain dominant, or would you consider yourself more multi-dominant, possessing both strong left brain and right brain qualities? Can we become more multi-dominant if we want? Would that mean we are using more brainpower? The answers to the last two questions are yes.

Tony Buzan, author of the book *Use Both Sides of Your Brain* and leading authority on learning, developed pioneering techniques to facilitate greater brainpower. Buzan explains our brain's innate programming for using both sides of our brain, relaying that the left and right sides of the brain are not simply two connected structures with different characteristics, but rather they are two structures each containing facets of the other's abilities. The brain is synergistic; when we encourage the development of a weaker mental area, that is, for example, intuitive thinking in someone driven more by logic, not only does the non-intuit become more intuitive, but other mental abilities seem to improve as well.[6]

The Power of Synergy

From what Buzan describes, we see that our brains are driven by collaboration. Our behavior is the end result of that collaboration. While specific parts of the brain have primary responsibility for specific functions, it is the interaction of those diverse functions that enables us to behave as we do.[7] While our brain is set up for synergy and the potential is there to use, in Buzan's words, "both sides of our brains,"[8] many of us do not tap into our natural potential. We are instead constrained by our preferences; we form behavioral habits.

We carry these same habits and constraints over to our work. At work, we have owners and specialists for departments, initiatives, projects, and tasks, just as the brain has functional owners. The expectation is that our work groups will function as interdependently as the brain does. We find more and more, though, that individuals and groups are working in isolation, or we work around each other to get our results. Individuals and groups that work collaboratively are lately the exception, not the rule. Why the shift away from collaboration? Shorter cycle times, more aggressive reporting demands, and keeping up with e-mail, voice mail, Black-Berries, and Palms force us into solitude. It is easier and faster to just do it ourselves. If the brain's synergies always have and always will net it greater intellectual power, then greater synergies among our people always have and always will net us similar power to achieve results.

Learning, the Brain, and Diversity

Not only is our brain synergistic, its potential is enhanced by diversity. Put another way, our brain's capacity grows through novel learning. The concept is simple: learning stimulates our brain. Whenever we experience new sights, sounds, tastes, and smells, use different muscle groups, read new words or languages, or listen to different perspectives, the brain responds favorably. Novel learning is our brain's best medicine. Renowned popular doctors Michael Roizen and Mehmet Oz, in their blockbuster book You: The Owner's Manual, explain that learning new things exercises the brain in such a way that it keeps it younger. They also tell us that we do not necessarily need to master the new learning to get the brain benefit. Pushing our mind into uncharted territory is stimulation enough.[9] It has been further suggested that when we use our brains to do new and different things, we increase its own processing options thereby making us more able to deal with change.[10] Conversely, our brain being locked in a habitual pattern makes it harder for the brain to embrace novelty.[11] To allow the brain to be more open to something different, some momentary letting go is needed. We saw one example of letting go with the assertive leader who engaged in a creative reflection. Let's look at another example of letting go.

Imagine that you are on a business trip to a country you have never been to before, for example, Switzerland. You are a "left-brainer." You are practical, focused, and talkative. As a courtesy, your business host offers to take you on a boat trip around one of Switzerland's stunning lakes. You arrive at the tour boat, and the lake and surrounding area look like a virtual postcard. The water is glistening. There are snow-capped mountains in the distance. Vineyards line the hillside. The tour boat is impeccably clean, well maintained, and operating to a precise time schedule.

Here you have a perfect opportunity for a brain workout; everything around you is new. According to what we know, what would you, the left-brainer, typically focus on? Your first inclination would be to retreat to your preferences. You would focus on the well-maintained boat and precise time schedule. You would be talking a lot, making comments about how you appreciate the order and the structure. You would be thinking, "I wish our company ran like this boat!"

Instead, try letting go of your preference, just for the boat ride. You need to move from left to right brain focus. You could try any one of the following: sit quietly and let your mind wander or daydream. Take in the landscape. Look at objects you have never seen before. Listen for new sounds or pay attention to new smells. Since many of the other passengers could be from a foreign country, speaking a foreign language, you could read their facial expressions and body language. You could also try a new food or drink. Any of these actions would move your brain away from the habitual, open it up to new learning, and activate the brain overall.

We talk a lot about diversity in the work world. Companies make it a point to bring in new blood to stimulate results, but ask yourself this: do we really make the best use of diversity in our ranks? Diversity in ideas, styles, experiences, and perspectives is welcome in thought but constrained in practice in most work settings. I could cite countless examples of individuals being brought into a team for their different perspectives and then held back from bringing their contributions to the forefront. In fact, such individuals usually end up being referred for coaching to help them assimilate when, in fact, it is the team who should be coached to take advantage of the new person's perspective.

While the intention is good, the fact remains that in most social networks, the work world being one of them, managing diversity is difficult. Perhaps one way for you as a leader to learn to better leverage diversity in your teams is to first learn to better leverage it in yourself, using your own development as the working model. In learning to let go of your preferences and access alter-brain behaviors, you will have a process to help you do just that.

The Brain's Check and Balance

The brain is part of a larger structure, the central nervous system (CNS). The CNS consists of the brain and the spinal cord. The CNS is arranged in a physical hierarchy with structures at the top carrying out more complex duties than those located at lower levels. Sound familiar? This is how organizations are structured. Higher-ranking executives are on the top floors, and the ranks cascade down from there. Our brain, like our top leaders, processes, directs, and informs, while the spinal cord carries the brain's information to the organs and muscles of the body. At work, those who report to us are our spinal cord, relaying information to us as well as down into the organization. The CNS is also instrumental in something precious to leaders, sleep. Leaders with demanding travel schedules experience CNS disruption when they are jet lagged. Jet lag is a function of a disruption in circadian rhythms (regularly recurring biological patterns); this disruption causes CNS structuring to poorly regulate sleeping, calm, and arousal. This CNS disruption is passed on to our secondary nervous system, the peripheral nervous system (PNS).

The PNS has two divisions, the autonomic and the somatic. The somatic nervous system (SNS) controls the movement of skeletal muscles and transmits information about touch, pain, and temperature to the CNS. The autonomic nervous system (ANS) controls the body's involuntary functions and regulates activity and recovery.[12] The ANS is where your body regulates its performance and rejuvenation. As such it is our body's check and balance. The ANS itself has two divisions, which impact the organs of the body in opposite ways. For example, one part of the ANS, the sympathetic division, accelerates heart rate, while its counterpart, the parasympathetic division, slows it down. The sympathetic division is the body's activation arm, allowing it to respond to emergencies, stressful situations, and the demands of an active workday. The parasympathetic division comes into play to help the body digest, store energy, and rest.[13] In the earlier reference to jet lag, the sleep disruption that began in the CNS is experienced by the PNS as a rest disturbance.

The collaboration you see evidenced in our two nervous systems shows again the dynamic interplay through which our brain functions. There is a continuous and naturally fluid exchange that keeps our bodies and minds regulated and functioning at their best. As leaders, we too must constantly ebb and flow in our behavior between right and left brain abilities in order to be at our best.

Stress and Emotions

"All Stressed Out"

When we encounter stressful events it is more difficult to move between right and left abilities. It is easier to retreat to our preferences. Think about your day-to-day tasks and interactions. On most days you are able to reason and perform as needed. You can more readily push yourself and perhaps entertain different perspectives. Certain external factors, however, can compromise our brain's ability to function and to extend itself. Stress is one such factor. The interesting thing about stress is that it has the potential to both compromise and enhance our brain's abilities, meaning that stress can shut us down or spur us to become even better. The more you understand about the nature of stress, the more likely you are to have the latter occur. You will also be better able to shift your style even in the face of stress.

There are two kinds of stress: acute stress, which is something short-lived occurring in the moment; and chronic stress, resulting from repeated or prolonged difficult circumstances. I began my consulting work almost twenty years ago specializing in clinical factors affecting leaders. One of those factors was stress. Many of my coaching assignments centered on helping clients better manage their stress. Today, we tend not to look at stress in isolation as something to manage, but rather we try to help individuals build better overall adaptive responses and resilience. Understanding the stress response is a necessary precursor to both adaptability and resilience.

The body is typically stimulated by short-term stress.[14] Short-term stress has been found to stimulate the immune system. Long-term or repeated stress, however, affects us negatively. While each of us has different stress tolerances, we are all set up to mobilize for brief stress and to then recover. When stress is recurrent or prolonged, we become overtaxed and problems begin to arise.[15]

Stress has been described as a chain of physiological and psychological events that triggers a disruption in the body's homeostasis. The term "homeostasis" describes the process by which the body maintains functions necessary for biological life. Stress can be any event, positive or negative, that demands the body to readjust. This chain of events was first named by Walter Cannon as our fight-or-flight response. It is our body's way of preparing us to stand and fight or to flee during stressful times. The negative impacts of prolonged or repeated exposure to stress can surface in a number of ways. Physical symptoms occur in organs of the body, such as the heart or stomach. Our immune systems are also compromised during times of prolonged or repeated stress, as are areas of our bodies that are already vulnerable.[16] Stress-related symptoms can also be psychological or cognitive, such as nonspecific anger, anxiety, insomnia, depression, memory loss, or difficulty making decisions.

Stress is inevitable, especially for leaders. The goal of leaders should be to understand the nature of their stressors, along with both their reactions and their vulnerabilities, so they can develop better resilience. Stress should not be ignored or tolerated. It needs to be respected as one of our internal forces to be reckoned with.

The Emotions of a Leader

I was in the office one Friday at the end of the day. I was preparing to leave for a long holiday weekend and made the mistake of checking my e-mail *just one last time*. There they were: three messages about a problem I thought had been resolved earlier in the day. Under those three troubling e-mails was a new message, an attempt to dump on an unsuspecting victim—me. My initial thought was, "Wrong person, wrong timing." My thoughts quickly escalated from there. "What was he thinking? Did he really see this as my problem? And by the way, sending it to me at the eleventh hour was just irritating!" This situation represents one of those defining moments for a leader: how to use emotion to enhance rather than bury you.

Emotion is a complex brain experience involving multiple brain structures.[17] Our right hemisphere is dominant for emotional expression and for emotional recognition. Our frontal lobe is involved both in how emotional information is used in decision making and in impulse control.[18] Fundamental to our emotions is the brain's limbic system, a grouping of brain structures first identified in the early 1930s, with the term "limbic system" being coined decades later. Since then, we have refined our knowledge and understanding of our emotional drivers.[19]

In 1995, psychologist Daniel Goleman detailed that knowledge with his groundbreaking theory of emotional intelligence, marking a new way of thinking about our capability. In his book *Emotional Intelligence: Why It Can Matter More Than IQ*, Goleman teaches us about the workings of our emotional mind and proclaims that emotional intelligence, more than general IQ, is a precursor to success in work and in life. As Goleman explains, our higher brain—which gives us the ability to think—and limbic system—our ability to feel—have developed an intricate working relationship of dual leadership. In the day-to-day the higher brain, or rational mind, leads emotional response, but when a situation is intensified the limbic system, or emotional brain, takes charge. There is not only duality in leadership between day-to-day and high-intensity events, but there is also dual leadership within a heightened emotional event itself. When first confronted with an emotionally charged matter, our limbic system and, in particular, the amygdala (a key part of the limbic system) reacts. Our higher brain then comes in and processes what occurred, to finalize or at times second-guess our initial reaction. At times, the first response may be as intense as the experience itself; we could overreact. Goleman refers to such an overreaction as an amygdala hijack.[20]

In my experience with the late-day flurry of difficult e-mails, my initial reaction could have been to fire off a strained response to the person who annoyed me. This would be my emotional mind and, in particular, my amygdala hijack at work, a classic overreaction. The rational mind would then come in to discern what in the heat of the moment I had written that I might need to recant.

While outward emotional reactions may vary greatly from person to person and from one situation to the next, the role of the amygdala and the process of dual leadership are consistent. When we fail to acknowledge our brain's iterative emotional process, we run the risk of defending our overreactions. If we accept and leverage our brain's dual emotional leadership, we can develop better insight, self-control, and wisdom. Luckily for me, on that day self-control and wisdom prevailed. I replied: "Just got your e-mail. I'm on my way out; back in on Tuesday. Give me a call and we can talk through this." I was able to shift my style during a stressful situation from one of closure to the open-ended. My preference is to wrap things up. I am less comfortable leaving things undone. When stressed I could have a tendency to move for closure even more quickly than usual. Shifting style, while more difficult in heated moments, is precisely what is needed. In this case it afforded me a more prudent and enhancing option.

Anger: Emotional Asset or Detriment?

Anger is a healthy emotion. Feeling angry or frustrated is a signal that things are not going as one had hoped. Things do not always go as planned for leaders. People do not follow through. Deadlines are missed. Quality can suffer. At those moments when a leader is driving toward a goal and a setback arises, anger can be evoked. How a leader chooses to express anger has a dramatic effect on outcomes. Anger can be expressed in ways that spur others forward in productivity or bring them to a halt.

Aggression is an expression of anger that violates others, that sets them back. Science has placed a great deal of emphasis on understanding negative emotions. As far back as 1872, Charles Darwin wrote that rage was a response to a threat, and threats arouse individuals to defend themselves.[21] This is an important point, that anger is a response to a threat, and that threats arouse defensiveness. Think of the last time you got angry. If you got defensive, chances are you dug in your heels and closed off your mind. Remember though, you have two minds working for you, the initially aroused emotional mind and the more objective rational mind. Social psychologist Carol Tavris views human aggression in terms of choices, believing that we each have the ability to choose how we react to our anger. Tavris suggests that paying close attention to the meaning our anger has for us is key to both self-control and resolution. Tavris' perspective asks us to build our rational mind into our anger equation.[22]

Goleman's descriptions of how the higher and lower brains interact during high-intensity moments and how our amygdala can hijack us tell us that we are vulnerable when it comes to our emotions. Goleman's model of emotional intelligence says that emotional self-awareness gives rise to better emotional self-control. Tavris' perspective on anger is in line with Goleman's. Both believe that understanding our emotional monsters, so to speak, will open up rather than lock down our brain's emotional process. We will be left with more choices and less fallout and, more to the point, greater ability to exercise conscious style shifts that will extend our impact at times when it matters most.

The Social Leader

In 2006 Goleman jolted us once more, describing our brain's design to be social. In his terms, we are "hard-wired" to connect. He coined the term and theory of social intelligence. Goleman explains that social intelligence encompasses two specific skills. The first is social awareness, which involves reading others accurately and understanding the interpersonal world around you. The second social intelligence skill is social facility, which means acting on your social awareness in a way that promotes positive interactions.[23]

Goleman's thinking about our social brain is critical to leaders. Consider the following example: this leader sees himself as a fair, personable individual. He believes in honesty and integrity. He is well-intentioned and wants what is best for himself and his people. He believes that he knows his people well and that he has keen insights about the greater organization and the context of his work. This leader seems to want to do the right thing. He seems to possess social awareness. The problem, though, is that he tends to get caught up in the daily pressures, problems, and deadlines. His demeanor can be abrupt, overbearing, and at times harsh. His people often feel overshadowed, insecure, and frustrated.

In Goleman's terms, this leader may have good social awareness. He may understand his people and the greater social landscape, but he lacks the ability to act on that awareness. His actions are not informed by his social awareness. To his credit, he is halfway to leveraging his social brain. If we trust what science is telling us, this leader's good intentions are not being realized because the ultimate brain-to-brain social connections with his people are negative. The social experience—what the brains of those around him are connecting to—is negative. He needs to take what he knows and feels about his people and the work and communicate it back to them, fostering interactions that others can respond to favorably. He would need to shift style from driving the work to driving the social dynamic.

This example reflects a common leadership problem: leaders who believe that their good social/emotional intent is felt by their people. Leaders who think this way are focused on the work. They are very much intellectually disposed—inside their heads—rather than externally focused on the nature of their interactions. They, like the leader in the above example, are well-intentioned but not acting with social facility. In effect, these leaders are being undermined by their social brains and do not know it. The question to ask yourself is: what impact do my preferred styles have on my social connections, and how could certain style shifts help create better ones?

Executive Summary: Leadership and the Brain

1. While our brain is organized into specific structures, each with areas of primary responsibility, our behavior is the result of a complex interplay among those structures and functions. Our brain's structure and function is the perfect operating model for organizations and leaders.

2. The brain is divided into two hemispheres: the left and the right. Each brain hemisphere controls specific preferences in thinking and behaving.

3. The left hemisphere is our grounded tactician, able to plan, reason, and execute in the moment.

4. The right hemisphere is our strategist, innovator, and visionary. The right hemisphere is also dominant for emotional expression and recognition.

5. We have the ability to develop strengths in both left and right brain characteristics, to become multi-dominant.

6. Leaders can develop their multi-dominance by engaging alter-brain (diverse) behaviors and experiences.

7. Novel learning stimulates the brain to develop greater overall potentials. Both novel learning and diversity encourage the brain's natural synergistic process.

8. Being open to diversity is not easy. We tend to be creatures of habit. If you can practice momentary letting go of behavioral habits, you will increase your brain's diversity and gain greater alter-brain breadth and depth.

9. Stress and high-intensity moments can curtail our ability to extend beyond our preferences and/or cause us to overreact. Understanding our brain's emotional process along with gaining insight into our emotional reactions can enable us to better shift style when we need it most.

10. The nature of our interactions is now seen as pivotal to leaders' success due to recent findings about our social/emotional brain. Extending beyond our

preferences can assist us in creating more enhanced social connections in the face of today's work climate.

What has been introduced thus far is a perspective on what today's leaders are up against, along with an understanding of how our brain can be our greatest ally. You have met four leadership cases and have been introduced to a new concept to help broaden your leadership impact—the concept of alter-brain behaviors.

What we want to focus on in particular is how our knowledge of the brain equates to the behavioral skills a leader needs to possess in order to be effective. There are two premises here. The first is that we operate from constricting preferences and that style shifts are needed to lead more fully. The second premise is that organizing leadership behavioral skills according to how the brain is structured, using right and left hemisphere abilities along with integral interpersonal functioning, will enable leaders to make the needed style shifts and develop in sync with how their brains work. The next chapter will examine a leadership model equated to the brain's dual and synergistic nature. Ten specific guiding behaviors (behaviors leaders should follow in order to be most effective) will be presented, along with a process for developing greater leadership breadth and depth. Greater leadership breadth and depth comes through a more complete application of those guiding behaviors.

CHAPTER 2

THE MODEL

Yesterday I dared to struggle. Today I dare to win.

—Bernadette Devlin

The Right Brain / Left Brain Leadership Model was created to guide your ongoing development as a leader. It will help turn your struggles into gains and afford you more substantive results both personally and professionally. The model is all-inclusive, meaning it covers a full spectrum of behaviors a leader needs to make an impact. It enables you at any given point in time to assess your leadership abilities and chart a development course.

Right Brain/Left Brain: Counter-Intuitive

As you begin to familiarize yourself with the model and how it can help you, first consider the model's title. As the title reflects, the model is built around our right and left brain abilities, drawing on our brain's dualistic and synergistic nature. But why right brain / left brain leadership and not the other way around? The title and orientation of the model seem counter-intuitive—that's intentional! While we orient from the left, we need to lead from the right. The right brain in essence focuses on the future, while the left brain hones in on present realities. From a leadership perspective, leaders need to first look forward to the desired state in order to then tend effectively to the day-to-day.

Next, you will need to have a working understanding of the behaviors the model is built around. The model's ten behaviors were referred to at the close of Chapter 1 as "guiding behaviors," those charting the path for leaders to follow. These guiding behaviors were actually presented in Chapter 1 in the leadership assessment exercise. They are terms that you no doubt already use in the context of your work, behaviors conveyed in the language of leadership but conceptualized differently and more fully detailed here. To refresh your memory those behaviors and their definitions follow.

Transformational: to drive change in cultures, teams, and individuals relative to values, thoughts, and actions

Strategic: to be proactive and visionary; to have the long-range view

Savvy: to sense and respond appropriately to the organization's cultural climate; to get things done in a way that advances both you and those individuals and organizations you are affiliated with

Innovative: to have an open mind and be able to think creatively without restraint

Expressive: to clearly communicate your thoughts both formally and informally while providing the necessary context

Engaging: to understand and work well with others; to validate, involve, and recognize others, and to help them take on responsibility

Resilient: to possess the optimal physical and mental functioning, stamina, and mindset

Methodical: to plan well; to be systematic and effectual in your approach to initiatives

Grounded: to act with integrity, consistency, and stability; to be the steward and the gauge

Assertive: to be upfront, direct, and determined in order to get the desired results

Figure 2.1 shows the guiding behaviors sorted by right and left brain ability, along with two auxiliary behaviors. When leading from the right brain, behaviors are **strategic**, **innovative**, **transformational**, and **engaging**. When leading from the left, behaviors are **methodical**, **expressive**, **grounded**, and **assertive**. **Resilient** and **savvy** are auxiliary behaviors. They are right- and left-brain enhancing, supporting your leadership abilities by tending to you personally. **Resilient** contributes to your health, well-being, and staying power. **Savvy** speaks to your image and ability to negotiate the ever-so-crucial cultural landscape within your organization.

A Leader's Positioning: Looking Out, Looking Over, Looking In

The Right Brain / Left Brain Leadership Model is organized around three skill sets: the right brain skill set, the left brain skill set, and a support skill set. These three skill sets can be thought of as views leaders assume relative to their work. The right brain skill set assumes the view

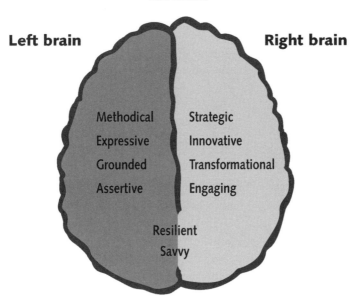

Left brain

Methodical
Expressive
Grounded
Assertive

Right brain

Strategic
Innovative
Transformational
Engaging

Resilient
Savvy

Figure 2.1 Guiding Behaviors Sorted by Right and Left Brain Ability

of *looking out* to the future, to a desired state you are moving toward. When you are *looking out* you are seeing beyond the day-to-day to upcoming challenges and opportunities, whether they be a month or a year from now. It is your long-term focus. The left brain skill set assumes the view of *looking over* the work. When you are *looking over* you are organizing, monitoring, and driving the work in progress. It is your near-term focus. The support skill set directs your inward focus, assuming the view of *looking in* at one's own fortitude and influence. While ten guiding behaviors comprise these three skill sets, each behavior is also broken down into ten traits. The ten traits for each guiding behavior show the complex nature of the behaviors, each having many nuances to consider. You may have been told for example that you were or were not strategic, but what does that really mean? By examining yourself in the context of the Right Brain / Left Brain Leadership Model's behavior **strategic** and its ten corresponding traits, you will be better able to discern precisely what that feedback meant and, more importantly, how to use the feedback as either a validation of ability or an indicator of a development need. All in all, with ten guiding behaviors and ten corresponding traits for each behavior, you have at your disposal 100 ways to develop breadth and depth as a leader.[1]

Leading from the ten behaviors in concert facilitates the synergies our right and left brains are capable of. Once you develop facility with the model and can lead from all three skill sets, you will not only be leading with great breadth and depth, but you will also be leveraging optimal

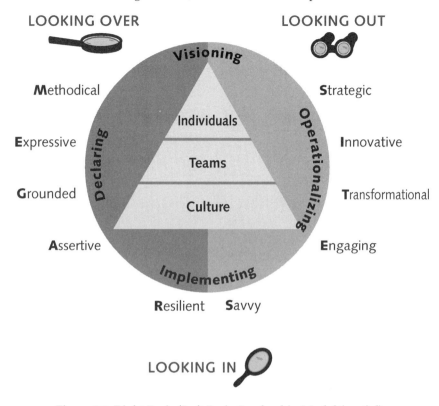

Figure 2.2 Right Brain/Left Brain Leadership Model (partial)

brainpower. Figure 2.2 shows the model. Note the three skill sets: looking out, looking over, and looking in. Note the ten guiding behaviors: **strategic**, **innovative**, **transformational**, **engaging**, **methodical**, **expressive**, **grounded**, **assertive**, **resilient**, and **savvy**. In addition to the skill sets and ten guiding behaviors, you will see a pyramid with the words "culture," "teams," and "individuals." These refer to a leader's target audiences. Finally, along the perimeter of the circle are four words representing the key processes a leader works from. Following, a leader's target audiences and key processes are explained in greater detail.

A Leader's Context: Four Key Processes

While the ten guiding behaviors represent the "how to" of leadership, the four key processes represent "what." The Right Brain / Left Brain Leadership Model identifies four key processes, those which are the very nature of a leader's work. These straightforward processes reflect the leader's context, or the circumstances within which your work occurs.

Shown in Figure 2.2, the four key processes include visioning, operation-alizing, implementing, and declaring. Leaders conceptualize their work around a mission and direction; this is their visioning. Leaders operation-alize their work by developing plans and allocating resources. Leaders implement their operational plans by driving for results. Leaders make declarations based on a culling of best practices and by identifying areas for change and improvement.

Of the four key processes, the first three are readily adopted as routine practice. Visioning is driven by the organization's strategic planning process. Operationalizing is the offshoot of the strategic plan, how we will actually execute the work. Implementation, attaining one's goals, is the basis for performance measures and, therefore, our main focus. Declar-ing, however—taking the time to reflect on what is working and what isn't—tends to occur sporadically and most often on the negative side. A problem occurs and we investigate in order to lessen the likelihood of it happening again. When motivated to make improvements, we research and reflect on the best of the best to learn from them. True declaring, how-ever, is a regular process of reflecting on the work to call attention to what we are doing well and what we need to improve on. It is about regularly sharing success stories and openly discussing failures. It is about going back over our work so that it can inform our next steps.

Effective leaders are in continuous and complete engagement with these four processes, moving from visioning to operationalizing to implement-ing to declaring. These four processes are dynamic. As you move from one to the next, your work context is ever-changing; therefore, you need to adjust course continuously along the way. Given this dynamic nature, the more diverse your repertoire (the more leadership behaviors and traits you draw on), the more adept you will be. For leaders, and all of us for that matter, diversity equals flexibility and flexibility equals success.

A Leader's Audience: Culture, Teams, Individuals

The leader's target audiences—culture, teams, and individuals—are displayed at the center of Figure 2.2. Of these target audiences, culture is positioned as foundational. Troubling of late is the lack of forethought given to organizational culture. While many of the problems companies face stem from weak, undefined, or fragmented cultures, tending to cul-ture in today's work climate is a hard sell. Many of today's organizations focus their attention on individual performance, not on culture or teams. They detail *what* individuals are to accomplish and neglect giving attention to the *how*. Just as the Right Brain / Left Brain Leadership Model identifies both the what and how of leadership, so too should organizations identify not only what but also how the organization and all its parts should function and interrelate.

Most leaders would agree that culture is important. Strong operating cultures hold members of a group to certain core values and protocols and thereby align everyone around the goals. They create better forward momentum. The problem is that making time in today's climate for cultural development is getting harder and harder. What can be said to make this point and get your eye back on culture? To begin with, strong cultures enable members to be clear about what they are supposed to do and how they are supposed to do it. If having your people clear about expectations is important, then tending to culture will help. If having a collective awareness is important—that sense in all members of your organization that they are part of a unified and aligned group, that everyone knows how to relate to each other and interact—then tending to culture will help. Organizations with a strong operating culture follow prescribed team and leadership models. Team models provide interpersonal norms and processes, as well as role and goal clarity. They help groups work through problems and develop trust, candor, reliance, and alignment. Leadership models set forth specific standards for leading. They help an organization's leadership form a team of its own, one that portrays stability and consistency to the ranks. These are the many benefits derived from taking the time to develop strong culture in your organization.[2]

Another compelling reason to tend to culture and to teams is that organizations are increasingly structured around complex matrixes. When an organization is set up as a matrix, individuals are required to report to multiple bosses and to work within multiple primary work groups. Unlike hierarchical organizations, a matrix requires greater alignment up, down, and across the organization. Individuals, regardless of their level or role in the organization, need to be in lockstep across functional areas. Matrixes also require greater collaboration across multiple groups, roles, and functions. Strong cultures and strong teams promote both alignment and collaboration. Without established teams and unified cultures, matrix structures are less likely to be fully engaged.

The final appeal for why tending to culture is so vital lies in the very nature of the collective. When groups form, cultures are going to form whether organizations lead the effort or not. In fact, left undirected, cultures will grow like weeds. Group members will decide how to relate to each other on their own. It is the nature of groups to seek values and create norms to follow. In the absence of identified norms and values, underground cultures will form and manifest as bad habits. Once these bad habits take hold, they are difficult to eliminate.

Think for a moment about a problem or issue that plagues you at work, one that is people or behavior related. Chances are the problem is rooted in culture. With an increase in industry consolidations and today's short-term business focus, attention to culture and teams is mistakenly diverted. As companies continue to run to the near-term, managing to short-term results, investing in culture will continue to fall by the way-side. You as a leader will be left to deal with the fallout regardless. Set, cultivate, and sustain the culture necessary for your people to be success-ful, or continue to be undermined by subversive cultures operating at will around you. Whether your organization is willing to emphasize culture and team development or not, you as a leader will be well served by step-ping up and directing that development. By investing in culture you are saying, "This is who we are, this is what we do, and this is how we do it." By investing in teams you are making it a given that *we work together.*

In the absence of defined cultures and established teams, individual performance exists in isolation. Some individuals will do better than others. You as a leader will have to invest more time than necessary to bring underperformers along. When the work culture is defined and teamwork is made a cultural imperative, individuals are better poised for accountable, collaborative performance and you as a leader can address performance issues in a more expeditious manner. By rewarding behaviors that show alignment with and adherence to the desired culture, that culture will become more firmly established. Business leaders and authors Larry Bossidy and Ram Charan describe the link between rewards and culture change by saying, "The foundation of changing behavior is linking rewards to performance and making the linkages transparent. An organization's culture defines what gets appreciated and respected and, ultimately, rewarded. It tells the people in the organi-zation what's valued and recognized, and in the interest of trying to make their own careers more successful, that's where they will concentrate."[3]

Effectively directing culture and teams as well as individuals will require both breadth and depth in leadership skills. Mastery of the guiding behaviors of the Right Brain/Left Brain Leadership Model and acuity in accessing alter-brain behaviors will help you possess these necessary skills.

A Leader's Actions: Right Brain/Left Brain Behaviors and Traits

Let's look more closely at the ten guiding leadership behaviors and their corresponding traits, beginning with right brain behaviors.

Right Brain Leadership: Leader's Line of SITE

Right brain leadership behaviors facilitate development of an organi-zation's desired state. The right brain behaviors *look out* to possibilities and from those possibilities identify opportunities for change. The acro-nym for the right brain behaviors is **SITE** (Strategic, Innovative, Transfor-mational, and Engaging). Right brain behaviors are a leader's Line of SITE. Line of SITE behaviors and their traits are detailed as follows:

Strategic: to be proactive and visionary; to have the long-range view. Strategic behavioral traits are:

- Intuitive
- Thoughtful
- Insightful
- Anticipatory
- Shrewd
- Big-picture oriented
- Global
- Holistic
- Theoretical
- Conceptual

Innovative: to have an open mind and be able to think creatively without restraint. Innovative behavioral traits are:

- Pioneering
- Risk-taking
- Playful
- Creative
- Novelty-seeking
- Imaginative
- Experimental
- Curious
- Spontaneous
- Unconventional

Transformational: to drive change in cultures, teams, and individuals relative to values, thoughts, and actions. Transformational behavioral traits are:

- Open to learning
- Assimilative
- Attuned
- Ambiguity-allowing
- Facilitative
- Opportunity-conscious
- Incremental
- Adaptive
- Mentoring
- Alignment-driven

Engaging: to understand and work well with others; to validate, involve, and recognize others, and to help them take on responsibility. Engaging behavioral traits are:

- Inquisitive
- Listening
- Respectful
- Responsive
- Inclusive
- Collaborative
- Empathic
- Empowering
- Charismatic
- Motivational

Left Brain Leadership: The MEGA Mind

Left brain leadership behaviors target the sheer volume of a leader's day-to-day tactical demands. The left brain behaviors *look over* to your in-the-moment planning, communicating, stabilizing, and driving. The acronym for these behaviors is **MEGA** (**M**ethodical, **E**xpressive, **G**rounded, and **A**ssertive). Left brain behaviors are your MEGA Mind. The MEGA Mind behaviors and corresponding traits are as follows:

Methodical: to plan well; to be systematic and effectual in your approach to initiatives. Methodical behavioral traits are:

- Task oriented
- Detail oriented
- Organized
- Effective
- Focused
- Procedural
- Sequential
- Logical
- Analytical
- Factual

Expressive: to clearly communicate your thoughts both formally and informally while providing the necessary context. Expressive behavioral traits are:

- Prepared
- Articulate

- Coherent
- Concise
- Erudite
- Presentable
- Passionate
- Personable
- Persuasive
- Interesting

Grounded: to act with integrity, consistency, and stability; to be the steward and the gauge. Grounded behavioral traits are:

- Composed
- Approachable
- Genuine
- Pragmatic
- Cautious
- Questioning
- Stable
- Loyal
- Established
- Trustworthy

Assertive: to be upfront, direct, and determined in order to get the desired results. Assertive behavioral traits are:

- Purposeful
- Confident
- Tenacious
- Driven
- Delegating
- Decisive
- Courageous
- Candid
- Confrontational
- Closure-seeking

 The Plus Factors

The final skill set consists of two guiding leadership behaviors referred to as the Plus Factors. The Plus Factors are right- and left-brain enhancing and *look in* at both your internal fortitude and your external influence. The Plus Factors, **resilient** and **savvy**, are described as follows:

Resilient: to possess the optimal physical and mental functioning, stamina, and mindset. Resilient behavioral traits are:

- Positive
- Emotionally sound
- Clear thinking
- Tolerant
- Flexible
- Spiritual
- Physically fit
- Fulfilled
- Relaxed
- Environmental

Savvy: to sense and respond appropriately to the organization's cultural climate; to get things done in a way that advances both you and those individuals and organizations you are affiliated with. Savvy behavioral traits are:

- Astute
- Subtle
- Diplomatic
- Promotive
- Timely
- Culturally oriented
- Networking
- Assimilating
- Coalition-building
- Visible

Figure 2.3 shows the full working model. In addition to detailing the behaviors of the MEGA Mind, Line of SITE, and Plus Factors, the figure shows connecting lines that extend from the right to left brain behaviors, illustrating possibilities for accessing breadth across skill sets. The connecting lines show ways in which you can ground yourself in a behavioral preference and access an alter-brain breadth behavior.

For instance, the MEGA Mind behavior **expressive** could reflect your preference. You may be someone with solid expressive skills. You are not, however, as adept at engaging others. You speak well and clearly, but when doing so, you are the center of attention. When one is engaging,

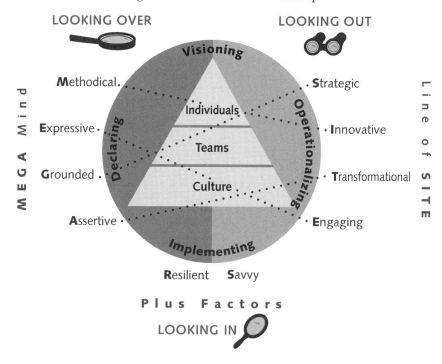

Figure 2.3 Right Brain/Left Brain Leadership Model

one uses communication to empower or motivate others. The focus with engagement is on those you are in dialogue with, rather than on you. Being expressive is a performance, whereas being engaging facilitates others. Think of the broader impact you would have if there were woven into your expressive abilities a dynamic interplay between you and those around you. Your style would shift between an internal and external focus. When focused internally, you would be establishing your power base. When externally focused, you would be bringing the contributions of those around you to the forefront. Look at the traits of engaging leadership: *inquisitive, listening, respectful, responsive, inclusive, collaborative, empathic, empowering, charismatic,* and *motivational.* Select one engaging trait and add it to how you express yourself. You could be motivational, making a statement that energizes others. You could focus on being respectful, being cognizant of your voice tone or facial expression in order to convey deference. Adopting traits of leadership behaviors across the model is how you develop greater alter-brain *breadth.*

If you wanted to develop alter-brain *depth* in a given behavior, rather than looking across the model you would look down the list of that behavior's traits. Staying within the behavior **expressive** consider that you are prepared, concise, and erudite, but not necessarily persuasive. You could devise a compelling argument to weave into your next presentation. This would be one way to add depth to your expressive ability. Depth development reminds us that each leadership behavior is complex and multi-faceted. It is not enough to consider yourself expressive because you possess some aspects of the behavior. You need to look within each behavior to its ten traits to assess yourself relative to the behavior's full range. Only then will you be able to assess yourself fully, and only then will you know how to develop in order to gain the maximum impact from a guiding behavior.

Development Tools

With this overview of the model clearly in mind, each leadership behavior will now be presented in greater detail. We will examine the full workings of the MEGA Mind, Line of SITE, and Plus Factors—behavior by behavior, trait by trait—by critiquing our four leadership cases, Angela, Ken, Madison, and Peter, and drawing from additional leadership exemplars. Specific tools will be offered to support our overarching developmental approach of shifting style, accessing alter-brain behaviors for breadth or depth. These tools will at times assist you in making a style shift to a different behavior or help you develop a new trait within a behavior. Tools may be specific to a given behavior or applicable across multiple right and left brain behaviors and traits.

These tools, like our guiding leadership behaviors, are either right brain, left brain, or supportive in nature. Right and left brain tools come from schools of thought in psychology. They emanate from how these theoretical perspectives view behavior and, therefore, how they approach behavior change. Right brain tools are based on humanistic and affective perspectives and focus on awareness, emotions, trial and error, the whole, the unstructured, and the new. The right brain tools you will be learning about include:

- Active listening
- Brainstorming
- Drawing
- Extension learning
- Journaling
- Reflection
- Summarizing
- Visioning

Left brain tools are based on behavioral and cognitive approaches and focus on logic, structure, associations, repetition, and steps. The left brain tools you will be learning about include:

- Behavior rehearsal
- Chaining
- Checklists
- Cuing
- Logging
- Planning aids
- Reframing

Several supportive tools are from the practices of wellness and nontraditional medicine, and one is an integrated brain tool leveraging right and left brain ability. The remaining supportive tools refer you to advisors (mentors) and subject matter experts (SMEs). While "SME" usually refers to a particular individual expert, for our purposes an SME will mean specific individuals, for example, an author whose book is recommended— or it will mean a broad body of relevant knowledge, for example, change management. This book's intent is to provide a full-spectrum model, one that in effect organizes the leadership knowledge base in an accessible way. Specific information incorporating my perspective about each guiding behavior will be included; however, the intent is to convey that the full breadth and depth of those behaviors could not and should not be covered by any one resource but rather through the integration of multiple sources. In order for you to reach maximum impact, you should consult additional and specific subject matter experts. You will be directed on how to do so, and certain resources will be suggested as being particularly relevant. Some resources will be referenced directly in the text. In addition, a list of books, a suggested leadership behavior library, will be provided toward the end of the book, offering a broader range of current resources. The supportive tools you will be learning about are:

- Attitude setting
- Deep breathing
- Energy recovery activities
- Feedback
- Feedforward
- Meditation
- Mentors
- Mind mapping
- Questionnaires

- Sensory aids
- Subject matter experts (SMEs)
- Values clarification

Over the next several chapters, each tool will be presented with an application in order to familiarize you fully with it. At the end of the book a complete listing shows each trait with the tools that can be applied to assist you with your development. In that way, for any trait you are looking to develop, you will know at least one specific tool you can use. Turning our attention to the right brain first, Chapter 3 takes us through the leader's Line of SITE.

CHAPTER 3

RIGHT BRAIN LEADERSHIP: LEADER'S LINE OF SITE

The best way to predict the future is to invent it.

—*Alan Kay*

In 1982 at the age of twenty-nine, Howard Schultz went to work for Starbucks, a Seattle-based company that at the time was in the business of selling coffee beans. Schultz's vision was to create the American version of an Italian espresso bar. Starbucks sold the operation to Schultz in 1987.[1] The rest is history. The future of the American coffee experience was reinvented. Like Schultz, the right brain leader gets beyond the present to invent and move toward future states. Right brain leadership enables us to vision, to create, and to change the world around us.

Right brain leadership is our starting point. While it is easy to become mired in the details of the day-to-day, leadership without forethought will put the work in charge of you rather than the other way around. Right brain leadership behaviors include one's ability to be **Strategic**, **Innovative**, **Transformational**, and **Engaging**. The right brain skill set, called the leader's **Line of SITE**, enables you to look out into the distance, bringing the long-range view clearly into focus. Comedian George Burns once said, "I look to the future because that's where I'm going to spend the rest of my life."[2]

This chapter will examine the four leadership behaviors of the Line of SITE, along with each behavior's ten corresponding traits. The four behaviors of the Line of SITE are defined as:

Strategic: to be proactive and visionary; to have the long-range view

Innovative: to have an open mind and be able to think creatively without restraint

Transformational: to drive change in cultures, teams, and individuals relative to values, thoughts, and actions

Engaging: to understand and work well with others; to validate, involve, and recognize others, and to help them take on responsibility

STRATEGIC

The future is the past through another gate.

—*Arnold Glasgow*

A good strategic leader is skilled at finding and choosing the right gate as Howard Schultz did. Strategic leadership is also about recognizing and mitigating potential threats. It is about moving the work culture from being reactive to proactive. Specifically, strategic leadership is defined as being proactive and visionary; to have the long-range view. How does one become a good strategic leader? The ten traits of **STRATEGIC** leadership are:

Intuitive – knowing things instinctively

Thoughtful – giving careful consideration

Insightful – seeing clearly into the nature of complex subject matter

Anticipatory – being aware of the imminent

Shrewd – being clever and preemptive

Big-picture oriented – taking extended aspects of a situation into account

Global – seeking input that generates a worldwide perspective and application

Holistic – taking all aspects of a situation into account

Theoretical – able to speculate

Conceptual – able to form parts into a whole

Intuition is at the top of the list. Consider the following excerpt from the teachings of Swami Dyhan Giten, an internationally recognized teacher and advisor to organizations. Giten's work centers around developing greater awareness in organizations and on the power of intuition. He says: "To see life from the perspective of intuition is to have vision. To see life from the perspective of intuition is like looking at life from the summit of the mountain, whereas seeing life only from the perspective of intellect is like looking at life from the foot of the mountain. Through learning to listen to our intuition, we learn to be in contact with the Whole."[3]

Intuition is the foundation from which strategic leadership emanates. To be intuitive means we are able to know something instinctively. We sense that it *could* be. A popular personality tool, the Myers-Briggs Type

Indicator (MBTI), tests for intuitive preferences. The MBTI looks at four scales, one of which is sensing. Sensing is a preference for taking in information through our five senses, noting what is actual, versus intuiting, a preference for taking in information through a "sixth sense" and noting what might be. Sensing is left brain in nature and intuition is right brain. If your preference is for sensing, you are more likely to think tactically and be grounded in present realities. If your preference is for intuitive thought, you see patterns, trends, and themes. You see future possibilities.[4] Accomplished strategic thinkers apply their intuition to the broadest possible levels, to the big picture, globally and holistically. They take their vision (what could be) and craft overarching approaches (strategies) to get there, considering the all-inclusive context.

Schultz's vision for Starbucks, the reinvention of the American coffee experience, was realized by his approach: to create a following for a brand image that blended Euro-style coffee drinking with diverse American lifestyles, tastes, and needs. The Starbucks strategy and resulting brand, in essence, blended its offering as masterfully as Starbucks blended its coffee beans and flavors. You could grab your coffee and muffin and go or drink-in in the trendy, hi-tech, yet relaxed cafés. More specifically, Starbucks would provide consistent, specially brewed and prepared coffee in an upscale environment, with stores close to the customer's base. Starbucks a la Schultz was a huge win, one that embodies strategic thinking. He needed to look out over trends, mindsets, and habits to determine if the world was ready for his concept. It apparently was.

Ken's Strategic Leadership

Turning to one of our leadership cases, we will examine how Ken fares as a strategic leader. As the new CEO of a growing nonprofit corporation, Ken's charge is to craft a five-year strategy for the organization's board. Ken is also expected to assess and change the culture of the organization in order to address its chronic issues impacting customer service and quality.

Ken came to his new CEO position with a reputation as one to get things done. He is *anticipatory* about issues that will need attention. He is *insightful* and *thoughtful* about setting the next course of action required, clearly discerning the nature of the situation and then giving careful consideration before acting. His *intuitive* grasp of what's needed and *shrewd* methods of implementation have helped propel him to his current level of leadership. He is also aided by his high score in *theoretical;* he is skilled at forecasting and speculation.

When it comes to being *big-picture oriented, global,* and *holistic,* however, we see that Ken is able to take a long-range view, but for Ken that view exists in a somewhat narrow scope. Ken can look at his organization and compare it to other similar organizations. He would benchmark to a national standard. Ken would less likely broaden his thinking outside of that vantage point to how other industries may inform his circumstance, even those similar or related, or to look worldwide for direction and insights. He also tends to look at distinct problems, at parts rather than at the whole. He struggles with being *conceptual*. Ken could benefit from developing the traits for assessing the broader realm of any situation.

Using Giten's analogy of the mountain, we would say Ken is more than halfway up the mountain looking out, but he is not yet viewing things from the summit. His strategic ability shows vision but lacks a broad-based perspective. A circle chart, shown in Figure 3.1, illustrates an assessment of Ken's strategic ability. Dots placed closest to the center of the circle represent low scores on the traits corresponding to strategic leadership. Dots closer to the outside of the circle represent higher ratings. Ken's strategic constraints are illustrated through lower scores on *big-picture oriented*, *global*, and *holistic*. In order for Ken to succeed at both his strategic plan and in crafting a vision and strategy for culture change, he will need to extend his strategic depth to lead from a broader platform.

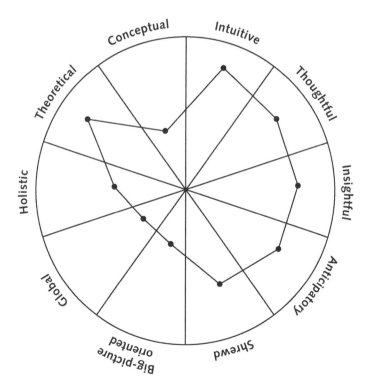

Figure 3.1 Ken's Ratings for Traits of STRATEGIC Leadership

Strategic Thinking Tools

Ken can use three tools to help him with strategic depth: extension learning, summarizing, and the mind mapping technique. Each of these activities aids in the development of one or more of the strategic behavioral traits.

Extension learning initiates an activity that extends your knowledge beyond its present scope. Ken should task himself to do an extension activity several times a month over the course of the next several months. He can use work or personal pursuits as his vehicle. Ken is a runner. He runs every day and with great discipline. He does so as his exercise regime. He could investigate activities that are an extension of his current exercise program, a different form of exercise, such as tai chi, a Chinese alternative exercise using mind focus and slow movement to promote muscle tone. Tai chi is thought to have multiple health benefits including mental calm and clarity.[5] Including an activity like tai chi as an extension learning would broaden Ken's fitness training perspective while developing his strategic depth. For Ken, this new exercise would give him a better big-picture and holistic perspective on health, that it is not only about cardio and strength training, but that there are mind-body components as well. Tai chi in particular would help him to think more globally as he learns about the contributions of other cultures to something that impacts him. It would further serve as a mindset shift for Ken from the grounded behavioral trait *established* to the innovative behavioral trait *unconventional*. As such, his alter-brain breadth would be impacted as well.

Summarizing, as a tool, here means starting a presentation or discussion by providing an overview before getting into the details. Summarizing would help Ken think more conceptually, from whole to part. Rather than focusing on the issue at hand, he could intentionally begin formal and informal conversations by laying out the full context of the circumstance, not just the related tasks. Summarizing has the added leadership benefit of promoting alignment, as individuals feel more grounded in the path forward.

Mind mapping would be of great value to Ken because it would help him think in a more all-encompassing manner, developing his holistic capability. Tony Buzan was referred to in Chapter 1 for his pioneering work in leveraging our brain potential. Buzan, inventor of mind mapping, created a technique which allows for a visual and nonlinear organization of ideas and images around a central thought. Mind maps allow the brain to think freely and more completely, and they have many uses. Ken can use mind mapping to address any key business challenge—for example, how to drive greater ownership in his organization. Buzan details how mind mapping is done in his bestselling book *How to Mind Map®: Make the Most of Your Mind and Learn to Create, Organize and Plan*.

Buzan's book is a powerful must-read for leaders wanting to improve both their right and left brain thinking.[6]

We have looked at the first guiding behavior and Ken's leadership challenges. A summary of that review follows. Summaries such as this one will be provided after each behavior and case critique as a way to distill the information and serve as guidance for your own development planning later on.

Ken's STRATEGIC Style Shift Summary

High scores: *Intuitive, thoughtful, insightful, anticipatory, shrewd, theoretical*

Alter-brain depth targets: *Big-picture oriented, global, holistic, conceptual*

Tools: Extension learning, summarizing, mind mapping technique

Alter-brain breadth impact: Extension learning will encourage a shift from **grounded** (trait *established*) to **innovative** (trait *unconventional*)

Extension learning and mind mapping tap into one's creative power. Creativity is an invaluable alter-brain enrichment. To learn more about the role of creativity in leadership we turn to the next Line of SITE behavior, **innovative**.

INNOVATIVE

> Every child is an artist. The problem is how to remain an
> artist once he grows up.
>
> —*Pablo Picasso*

The thing I missed most about going from kindergarten to first grade was that we stopped coloring. With each successive school year, art was more and more absent from learning protocols, replaced by scholastic pursuits. I did well in grade school and high school, went on to college and ultimately entered a doctoral program. There, on my first day in the program, my professor pulled out large sheets of flip chart paper and a box of crayons. She put on classical music and told us that we were going to create something with no words, only pictures. Far from my earlier days of comfort with crayons and finger paints, I was apprehensive at best. What I came to learn was a process to access different areas of our brain, those areas that are more creative. I was taught mind mapping and other creative activities to help me to innovate.

Perhaps the most interesting of today's leadership challenges is how to bring innovative leadership into our work. If leaders are driving for results and doing so from a near-term perspective, how can we stimulate creativity? There may well be a more pertinent question, though. Given the expectation to do more, do it faster, and do it with less, can we succeed without creativity? Consider the following:

> The frames of our mind create, define—and confine—what we perceive to be possible. Every problem, every dilemma, every dead end we find ourselves facing in life, only appears unsolvable inside a particular frame or point of view. Enlarge the box, or create another frame around the data, and the problems vanish while new opportunities appear. This practice we refer to by the catchphrase, **it's all invented.**[7]

This excerpt is from Rosamund and Benjamin Zander's book *The Art of Possibility*. The Zanders' premise is that we need not be confined by what exists or what we perceive to exist. We can invent a new reality for success. In order to do so we need to think in innovative fashion. The behavior **innovative** means to have an open mind and be able to think creatively without restraint. Creativity author Stephen Nachmanovitch is quoted as saying, "The most potent muse of all is our own inner child."[8] Whereas being strategic is to view life from the summit, being innovative is to view life from the eyes of a child, to imagine without the thought constraints adults are more prone to. The traits of **INNOVATIVE** leadership are:

Pioneering – forging new ground

Risk-taking – taking a chance

Playful – fun-loving

Creative – able to generate original ideas or constructs

Novelty-seeking – interested in the new or unknown

Imaginative – able to visualize and think about the unlikely

Experimental – being interested in trial and error

Curious – being eager to know

Spontaneous – living in the moment

Unconventional – being willing to consider the unusual

Madison: The Innovator

Of our four case studies, Madison is the most functionally **innovative**. Her job requires it. Let us examine how Madison measures up to the ten innovative traits. As creative director for a design team, Madison is continuing to nurture her lifelong artistic interest and ability through her career. Having lived both in a small west coast town and in New York City, she was exposed to diverse experiences and perspectives that served to nourish her innate curiosity and creativity. She is now known to be a creative talent with a fascinating imagination. She is also seen as good-natured, fun to be around, and always ready to seize the moment. As such, Madison scores high marks on the innovative traits *playful*, *creative*, *imaginative*, *curious*, *novelty-seeking*, and *spontaneous*. She is off to a great start as an innovative leader. Innovative traits Madison scores low marks on are *risk-taking* and *unconventional*. While her thinking is at the forefront of creativity, she prefers to take actions that are more proven. She is uncomfortable taking chances. She likes to play it safe and is fairly traditional. On the last two innovative traits, *experimental* and *pioneering*, Madison falls in the average range. She will test new ideas and methods and forge the path for fresh ways of doing things provided they involve minimal exposure.

Madison is a new leader with very few reference points for what good leadership should look like. Her parents are both professionals, but neither of them is in a creative field. When Madison looks to her parents as leadership models, much of what she sees is different from how those in her line of work think and act. Madison is unsure of how her innovative talent helps or hinders her ability to lead. Madison's ratings for the innovative traits are shown in Figure 3.2.

What do Madison's innovative ratings mean for her as a new leader? How should she direct her creative talent to her benefit? Madison's innovative strong suits can be applied to her leadership advantage in a number of ways. Her curiosity, imagination, and pioneering nature make her well disposed to facilitate and contribute to a range of strategic discussions. She needs to recognize and cultivate her inclination for creative problem solving, reinvention, and sorting future directions. These are skills more structured thinkers are sometimes hard-pressed to effect. While her left brain colleagues are making lists, she can be generating ideas and novel solutions. Both her creativity and playfulness can be motivational and inspirational in marking milestones and giving relief during stressful work times. The fact that she is imaginative yet traditional may bode well for her as a young leader. If she were more unconventional at this stage in her life, she may be perceived as less stable and less able to assimilate.

What, if anything, should Madison guard against? Are creative leaders at a disadvantage? Creativity, while a notable plus for a leader, can pose problems if one is not able to move from the unstructured to the structured. Like many creative leaders, Madison will need to know when to make that shift in style in order to be successful. She will need to shift style from right to left brain in order to be in command of the day-to-day. Madison is in fact already under scrutiny for not being able to focus, a sign that she is not yet making the needed style shift. Madison needs to realize when her creative strengths are, in essence, being overplayed. Otherwise, her overall impact will suffer. In addition, her low score on risk-taking is an issue that requires attention, because failure to take

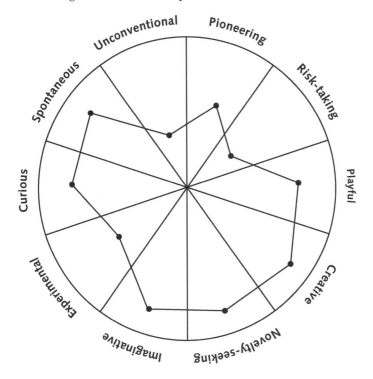

Figure 3.2 Madison's Ratings for Traits of INNOVATIVE Leadership

necessary risks is viewed by many as a leadership weakness. While she has great depth as an innovator, Madison needs to avoid overplaying her innovative strength while at the same time becoming more comfortable challenging the status quo.

Creativity Tools

Madison has two development opportunities. In essence, she needs to become more focused and less cautious. To develop better focus she can start in her natural preference, in her right brain, and use a trait that she is strong in, *novelty-seeking*, to help her. She can brainstorm ways that she and her team can become more focused. In brainstorming, thoughts are generated without structure. There are no right or wrong answers, no good or bad ideas. Put on some music, take out a large sheet of paper and some crayons or markers and begin. Make it a playful event, not an intellectual one. Madison's brainstorm session produced ten possible ways she could improve focus:

1. Tie a bright red ribbon around my finger to remind me to focus.
2. Start every day with a ten-minute focus huddle.

3. Write the word "focus" 100 times every night before I go to bed.

4. Set up my planner to send me a daily message about focus.

5. Get a focus mentor.

6. Start a breakfast club meeting once a week, bring in donuts or something good to eat, and gather the group to gauge their focus.

7. Have the word "focus" done in bright colors on a poster and hang it in the work area.

8. Assign a focus "cop," every week someone different on the team, who will see where our focus seems good or bad and report it to me.

9. Have a contest for the whole team to find an inspirational quote about focus. The quotes are anonymously entered and we'll all vote. The winner gets some great prize. The quote becomes the screen saver on all the office computers or put into little frames that go on everyone's desk.

10. I come up with some mantra about focus for the group.

Brainstorming, however, is only the starting point. Once Madison's novelty-seeking activity is complete, she would need to shift style again in order to properly scrutinize alternatives and determine the most feasible solution. She would move from the unstructured to the structured. She would look across our model to the MEGA Mind, to the behavior **methodical** for further assistance.

Brainstorming is an invaluable tool with limitless applications. My most memorable use of brainstorming helped me through a peer-relationship dilemma. I was tasked to work on a high-profile project with a colleague I struggled to find virtue in. He and I had a strained relationship at best. He antagonized me and in turn I competed with him. Now we were to work intensively together for three months. We would be relying solely on each other for the project's outcome, and how we performed was important to both our careers. Coming home from the office on the train after learning my new fate, I decided to brainstorm ways to deal with the situation. At first I was simply having some fun, but I noticed that I actually came up with a few good coping strategies. I took the activity more seriously and unearthed some ideas that surprised me. I identified several sound ways of working better with my nemesis. Brainstorming gave me the freedom of thought to work out my dilemma. Additionally, the playful mindset that brainstorming facilitates is advantageous during high-stress times. In my case, it helped me not take myself so seriously. Suddenly my colleague was not as bad as I had made him out to be.

A second tool that could help Madison is a reflection. A reflection can be done in a number of ways. The method used here draws on the principles of qualitative research, specifically on a research method called phenomenology. Phenomenology is the study of something or someone we experience. It involves reflection on our views, our perceptions, and our interpretations. It looks at our experiences and helps us become aware of and understand their nature and meaning.[9] Madison can use the reflective perspective of phenomenology to better understand the nature of her apprehension. As Madison becomes more aware of her apprehension, she will be in a better position to decide what to do next to address it.[10]

Reflections access the right brain. They provoke the insight through which, in Madison's case, she will better understand her risk aversion. Here's what she could do. Over the next few weeks, Madison would take three small risks. The risks can involve opportunities in or out of work. The aim is to uncover reflections, not to become better at risk-taking. The specific steps for this activity using Madison's circumstance would be:

1. Decide on a risk and take it. The risk should be small and manageable. It could be as simple as asking a question in a meeting where you would normally remain quiet. The reason for keeping risk small is that it will keep your threat threshold low and your mind more open to insight.

2. Have sheets of flip chart paper and some markers ready. Soon after taking the risk go to a quiet place and draw anything that comes to mind. There need not be structure to the drawing. The product could be a single drawing or a collage of images and words. Be sure to use images and not create a word list.

3. When the drawing is complete, look it over and begin to put words to what you have drawn. Jot down thoughts that come to mind. Looking back again at the drawing and what you have written, summarize your insights.

How is this exercise different from what you would normally do? Most of us would think about some behavioral need we have and move directly to trying to change the behavior. What Madison has done by exploring the nature of her behavior is come to understand it better. She then accessed the more unstructured part of her brain with a drawing about her discovery to uncover more. Typically, we would create a list—like the list we create for New Year's resolutions—all the things we are going to do differently to make us a better or happier person. Madison created images, not lists. Once the images were created, she reflected on them and began to jot down thoughts—still not a list, nothing with order or form, just free-flowing written thoughts. Staying with her right brain, from both the unstructured images and written thoughts she created she will now summarize insights. This final form of reflection should provide her with both a full appreciation of the behavior she is trying to change along with a feasible next step.

These tools, brainstorming and reflection, are effective ways for any leader to drive his or her development from a right brain perspective. Brainstorming helps us to think without restraint. Adding drawing as part of a reflection helps our mind to think more freely. Summarizing as part of a reflection relates back to strategic ability and helps us think more holistically. Both brainstorming and reflection give us additional information, positioning us better to know what our next steps should be.

Madison's INNOVATIVE Style Shift Summary

High scores: *Playful, creative, novelty-seeking, imaginative, curious, spontaneous*

Alter-brain breadth targets: Overplayed **innovative** ability requires style shift to **methodical** focus

Alter-brain depth target: *Risk-taking*

Tools: Brainstorming (using a right brain strength to help left brain development), reflection along with drawing and summarizing to develop risk-taking

Additional note: Moderate *pioneering* and *experimental* abilities will increase as *risk-taking* improves

---

Leap of Faith

Madison has begun to see where and how her innovative ability is facilitative to her leadership and where and how it is not. She has begun to form parameters in her mind for her evolving leadership style. She is fortunate in some respects because she is well-disposed to right brain thinking, in particular, innovative thought. Many of us have been socialized away from the creative. The context in which leaders function today gives us even less permission to innovate. We are too often constrained dealing with the amount and pace of the work to be able to step back and free our minds. The reality, though, is that if you force yourself to do that creative exercise, you will ultimately save time through much enhanced outcomes.

This section on innovative thought requires a leap of faith for those who do not typically think this way. You are being pushed here to believe—to believe in the power of innovation and in the contribution it can make to your work, to believe that creativity is alive and well in each of us, and to believe that through innovation you will reach new heights of success.

TRANSFORMATIONAL

> Change is the constant, the signal for rebirth, the egg of the phoenix.
>
> —*Christina Baldwin*

If you were asked to date the beginning of the modern U.S. civil rights movement, what would you say? Many say it was December 1, 1955, when Rosa Parks, an ordinary seamstress in Montgomery, Alabama, refused to give up her seat on a bus to a white passenger. She was arrested for her brave act and later quoted as saying, "The only thing that bothered me was that we waited so long to make this protest." A young local pastor, Dr. Martin Luther King Jr., touched by Rosa's act, aligned with her to form the Montgomery Improvement Association, whose first order of business was the boycott of the city-owned bus company. Their boycott lasted for 382—days, received international attention, and led to a Supreme Court decision that outlawed racial segregation on all public transportation.[11]

Transformational leadership is able to drive change in culture, teams, and individuals relative to values, thoughts, and actions. The ten traits of **TRANSFORMATIONAL** leadership are:

Open to learning – being interested in knowledge

Assimilative – bringing others together

Attuned – being keyed in to current realities

Ambiguity-allowing – able to deal with the uncertainties of change

Facilitative – operating as a catalyst

Opportunity-conscious – looking for appropriate opportunities

Incremental – working progressively, in small steps

Adaptive – able to change

Mentoring – able to teach and coach

Alignment-driven – helping unify others around directions and goals

Looking at the life and work of Rosa Parks in greater detail, we see her for the transformational exemplar that she was. Parks' activism began long before her famous bus incident. It was her life mission to end racial inequality. As a child raised in the deep South, she lived in fearful times. She made a conscious decision as a young woman not to be immobilized by her fear. Instead, she opted to learn what she could and use that knowledge to guide her in prudent action. She and her husband were vocal and devoted NAACP (National Association for the Advancement of Colored People) members attuned to their community, working tirelessly to improve the lives of those around them. Their advances came from small progressive steps. Though a graduate of Alabama State Teachers College, Parks only found work as a maid and seamstress, but teaching was in her blood. The bus incident presented an opportunity and Parks took it. Her long life of service to a cause was immortalized when at the age of seventy-five she opened the Rosa and Raymond Parks Institute for Self-Development in Detroit, Michigan. She published her first book in 1994, *Quiet Strength: The Faith, the Hope, and the Heart of a Woman Who Changed a Nation.* Parks passed away in 2005.[12]

What is noteworthy about Parks is her ordinary status and extraordinary contribution. Transformation is one of the most difficult challenges leaders face. It takes a certain mindset, certain skills, and hard work to effect change. Think of what we can learn from Rosa Parks about transformation. Think of how her actions can inform the changes we want to make at work and in life. Our case study, Angela, is expected to transform the mindset of her team in terms of how they view the business and how they view their work. What can Angela learn from Rosa Parks?

Angela as a Change Agent

Angela is the vice president of sales for a multinational company. With the company now for two years, she is seen as solid, trusted, and involved. She has good support across the organization. Angela reports directly to the CEO, who expects Angela to address what is perceived by the greater organization as a limiting mindset on the part of Angela's people. While many in the greater organization have begun to embrace a new cultural direction, Angela's team is clinging to the past. They have an external rather than internal focus, meaning they are convinced the problems the company faces could be corrected by changing its course rather than seeing that they are the ones who need to adjust. One noted weakness for Angela is that she avoids conflict, working around an issue rather than dealing with it head on. The conflict between Angela's team and the greater organization is going to pose a development challenge for her. Angela's ratings for the ten traits of transformational leadership are indicated in Figure 3.3.

Angela has many transformational strong suits. She rates high on the traits *open to learning, attuned, incremental, adaptive,* and *mentoring.* Her openness to learning is evidenced by her interest in an array of knowledge from facts, trivia, and historical perspectives to science and the full range of how to do different things. She is attuned and adaptive in her ability to key in to what is happening around her and shift course based on that information. She is one to move in small progressive steps rather than take on a lot quickly, and she is a great teacher and coach to her people.

Angela has an average rating on being *assimilative.* While she herself can adapt and she is a good mentor, her ability to bring others along is contingent on how willing they are. She has low scores on *alignment-driven, ambiguity-allowing, facilitative,* and *opportunity-conscious.* These low scores reflect how she is being undermined by her inability to deal with conflict and to confront. Whenever she attempts to broach the subject of change with her team, they react with pushback. Their pushback causes Angela to back down and look for ways around them. Her inability to deal with resistance compromises her ability to gain alignment, deal with the unknown, be a true catalyst, and look for appropriate opportunities.

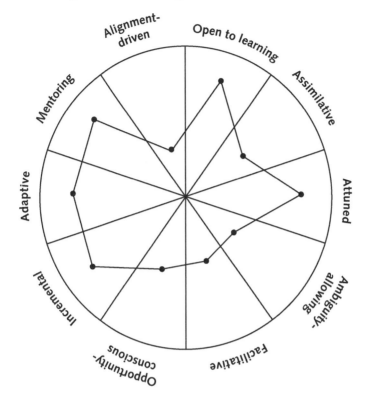

Figure 3.3 Angela's Ratings for Traits of TRANSFORMATIONAL Leadership

Resistance and the Nature of Change

A starting point for Angela is to better understand the nature of change itself. Change conjures up a host of reactions in those going through it. Many are fearful of what is coming. Some fear the unknown. Some are concerned about what they stand to lose. Change takes people out of their comfort zones. People respond with resistance, which is a natural, expected beginning to transformation.[13] Something else to understand about change is that the content of others' resistance contains critical information for a leader. The nature of their resistance helps a leader gauge how the change process is going. It can also alert the leader to potential risks or downsides. Leaders need to be listening to their people's resistance. Lastly, resistance can be lessened when leaders work to change the existing reward systems to align with new behaviors sought in a transformation.[14]

Angela has good relationships with her people. They trust her. She can use her relationships and personal demeanor to initiate discussions about the team's resistance. Her preferred behavior trait is *incremental*. This facility at planning and implementing work in stages is a skill she can leverage to hold these discussions, breaking them down into manageable experiences. Discussions could be organized in small groups or perhaps even as one-to-one meetings. They could be broken down further by themes, discussing one theme per session to lessen the likelihood that Angela will feel overwhelmed.

Chaining: Steps to a Goal

This means of organizing small progressive steps to reach a goal is referred to as chaining, creating a chain or link from one step to the next until you arrive at the desired outcome. Chaining can be used to develop any new behavior, like teaching a child to ride a bike. You break the experience down into attainable steps with each next step building on the previous one. Chaining works well when the goal you are trying to reach is challenging or complex. Breaking such a target down into manageable steps is a helpful way to get there.

Chaining is a left brain tool. The organizing and planning Angela will employ is left brain as well. Using her left brain chaining tool and left brain preference for planning will help Angela develop the transformational traits she is currently less adept at. Using her right brain ability of being attuned will help her know how and when to put her steps and plans into place. As such Angela will be effectively shifting style for maximum impact.

Angela can be inspired by what Rosa Parks was able to accomplish by combining small steps with seizing the right moments. Douglas MacArthur once said, "There is no security on this earth, there is only opportunity."[15] Parks would certainly agree. While Angela's opportunities need not be as confrontational as what Parks faced, she does need to develop being opportunity-conscious as an ongoing leadership trait. Furthermore, Angela can look across our model for assistance. As noted, she is a highly organized planner. She can use this left brain skill set in the behavior **methodical** to not only orchestrate discussions about resistance, but also, from a broader perspective, she can use it to craft a step-by-step plan that will move her people to where they need to be.

Reframing Perceptions

Angela is uncomfortable with the ambiguity that accompanies change. Her team's resistance is a large part of that ambiguity. For Angela to accept her team's resistance as a natural part of the change process, she is going to have to reframe it. She is going to have to see it as a good rather than an evil. In reframing, we use left brain logic to see things in a different light. We take an illogical thought, in Angela's case, the thought that resistance is bad, and reframe it to be a logical one: that resistance is part of the change process and therefore a sign of progress. In essence, we change the associations. Reframing changes a negative or counterproductive learned association into a positive, productive one.

To help Angela reframe her perception of resistance she can look again to her left brain preference for organization and conduct a structured activity. Doing so will ground her in her left brain preference for order and move her away from a perceived experience of chaos. One of the reasons leaders like Angela are overwhelmed with confrontation is they feel as though they are heading into the abyss. Such individuals can find solace in the order the left brain drives. By grounding herself in structure, Angela will be better able to reframe the matter of her team's resistance to change.

What Angela can do is get a clear glass jar and put it on her desk. In her drawer she will have ready a supply of bite-sized snacks. Each time she speaks with someone and his or her resistance is expressed, she is going to cue herself with the phrase "This is not a problem; this is good information," and listen to what he or she says. She is not going to try to change that person's opinion or address the mentioned issue. For now she is going to thank each person for bringing these thoughts to her attention. She will then reflect on what she heard and identify how the data informed her. When she goes back to her office she will add a number of snacks to the jar on her desk. The more valuable the information, the more snacks she will put in the jar. Each time the jar is full, she will gather in whoever is appropriate to share the payout—the snacks and her insights.

Doing an activity like reframing not only helps Angela begin to be more ambiguity-allowing, but it also takes the idea of transformation to a new level. She is calling attention to the change in a nonthreatening way. She is acknowledging resistance as a natural part of the process. She is having some fun while making the point that the change is underway.

Cuing: Prompting Change

While Angela may find assistance through reframing her perception, her conflict avoidance highlights an interpersonal issue that requires more directed attention. She could start with the same reflective experience Madison used to better understand her apprehension about risk-taking. A reflection exercise will help Angela understand the nature of her conflict avoidance, which limits her ability to be alignment-driven and assimilative. It is difficult to unify others around goals if you fear provoking a confrontation. Angela could also use a tool called cognitive cuing to assist her in bringing others together.

In the instructions for Angela's snack jar activity, Angela was told to cue herself using the phrase "This is not a problem; this is good information." This phrase served as Angela's signal to think differently. Our personalities and life circumstances cause us to develop certain thoughts, which lead us to certain behaviors or actions. One way to help us think differently and thereby act differently is to create a cue.

You can cue yourself using words, quotes, phrases, or symbols to prompt a different action, a desired forward movement. Angela could prompt herself to move through confrontation rather than around it. She could use a photograph that represents forward movement as her symbol, a waterfall, for example. She can have the photograph framed and put on her desk or wall to cue her to forward motion. Combining cuing with small incremental steps, Angela can work her way up to dealing with bigger and bigger confrontations.[16] Cues can be modified along the way to signify bigger and bigger steps. Soon she will be ready to be cued by an index card with the famous Rosa Parks quote, "I am not going to give up my seat," prompting Angela to stand her ground.

The cue itself, the words, quotes, phrases, or symbols by which something is represented, is left brain in nature. The left brain thinks in words and symbols. Making the cue tangible or concrete by writing a phrase on a piece of paper or using a photograph or an actual object to represent the cue is right brain in nature. The right brain thinks concretely, about that which is real, felt, or seen.

Dealing with confrontation is part of the left brain behavior **assertive**. Angela should more fully investigate the nature of assertiveness, conflict avoidance, and her own assertive traits to help her better shift style to this alter-brain behavior.

Angela's TRANSFORMATIONAL Style Shift Summary

High scores: *Open to learning, attuned, incremental, adaptive, mentoring*

Alter-brain depth targets: *Alignment-driven, ambiguity-allowing, facilitative, opportunity-conscious*

Tools: SME understanding of resistance to change and transformation, chaining, reframing, cuing, reflection

Alter-brain breadth targets: Style shift to **assertive** (trait *confrontational*)

Tool: SME understanding of assertiveness and conflict avoidance

---

The Art of Change

Transformations pose complex leadership challenges. Keeping the following points in mind will assist leaders in developing the art of change.

1. Resistance is a good thing. Resistance to change is normal and natural. It provides information to help you gauge how accurately people understand the

changes sought. It also helps you know who has and has not bought into the process. Embrace resistance, understand it fully, and deal with it.

2. Communication is a great thing. The three most important things in any change process are communication, communication, and communication. You cannot communicate enough. While there may be information you are not at liberty to share, there is much you can. Small details or facts may seem insignificant to you, but they are significant to your people. Communication helps break down the mystique surrounding change. It helps those experiencing the change feel more secure and better trust changes you are trying to make.

3. Validate loss. During any change process, individuals will naturally be preoccupied with what they believe they are losing. Many leaders think that if they focus on the losses, it will make it more difficult to gain buy-in. This is a faulty assumption. Reasoning with respect to change and loss is paradoxical; do the opposite of what your instincts tell you. By validating individuals' feelings of loss you will make them less resistant and more open to change.

4. Broadcast gains. While it is important to validate loss, it is equally important to keep benefits front and center. Leaders need to craft strategic communication messages about what individuals and the greater organization stand to gain. Be genuine. People's fraud antennas are heightened during transformations.

5. Help others cross the line. Ultimately, your success or failure during a transformation is dependent upon getting a certain number of individuals to cross the proverbial line. Beckhard and Pritchard refer to this in their book *Changing the Essence: The Art of Creating and Leading Fundamental Change in Organizations*, as getting to "critical mass."[17] Start with those closest to the line and bring them over first. Once they are secured, use them to bring the next group over and so on. You can also start with those most pivotal and work from there.

6. Seek evolution, not a revolution. The best change comes from evolution, not revolution. Start with small progressive steps and build from there.

7. Value history. Keep what works and what is near and dear whenever possible. Integrate rather than wipe the slate clean.

8. Look for and seize pivotal opportunities. If done correctly, seized opportunities become long-lived, celebrated milestones.

9. Promote a culture of learning. Make the act of learning as important as the act of doing as you move toward your desired state. Uncover and tell stories of successes and failures and validate both. While you are not seeking to invite mistakes, coach your people that during a change process mistakes can inform your success as much if not more than doing what is right.[18]

10. Get your ambassadors out there. Transformations are times when "strength in numbers" is the imperative. Leaders cannot effect change without educational assistance in the form of mentors, teachers, and coaches. Change is a time for learning, and learning requires educators. Identify, train, and discharge your change ambassadors.

The last point clearly speaks to the fact that change is accomplished only when you are able to enlist others in your quest. Our final right brain leadership behavior, engaging, is about just that.

ENGAGING

Leadership is the art of getting someone else to do something you want done because he wants to do it.

—Dwight D. Eisenhower

Pointed words by the late President Eisenhower, wouldn't you say? How does one go about influencing others in this manner? How does a leader appeal to her people in a way that brings out the best in them? The answer is through the art of engaging. Engaging leadership first and foremost involves understanding and working well with others. You must be able to show others that you validate their contributions. You must involve everyone, not just those who are more vocal. You must recognize others appropriately. Lastly, an engaging leader by virtue of his relationships and interactions is effective in enlisting others to take on their share of responsibility. The behavior **engaging** is defined as understanding and working well with others, validating, involving and recognizing others, and helping them take on responsibility. The traits of **ENGAGING** leadership are:

Inquisitive – probing further, especially into others' thoughts

Listening – paying attention for accurate understanding

Respectful – having consideration for others

Responsive – addressing the concerns of others

Inclusive – involving everyone

Collaborative – working along with others

Empathic – understanding others' perspectives

Empowering – giving responsibility to others

Charismatic – enthusing others through personal magnetism

Motivational – inspiring others in positive action

When we think of engaging leadership, we tend to equate it to being captivating. We think of heroes and icons that are admired for their allure, their charisma, or their accomplishment. Being engaging is in part about admiration, but there is more to it than that. Engaging leadership is about heroes making heroes. Engaging leadership is less about the awe one inspires and more about others' aspirations. Engagement is about connecting with others in a way that unlocks their potential, making them valued contributors.[19]

One popular contemporary personality who embodies engaging leadership is Dr. Mehmet Oz. Dr. Oz seeks to engage us to better our health. He has been seen on his Discovery Channel show, *Ask Dr. Oz,* and has appeared numerous times on *Oprah.* He is author and coauthor of various bestsellers about health and wellness, including the award-winning book *Healing from the Heart.* Dr. Oz is the 1999 recipient of the World Economic Forum's Global Leader of the Year award and was listed in *Healthy Living* magazine as Healer of the Millennium. He is professor and vice-chairman of surgery at Columbia University, director of the Integrated Medicine Center, and director of the Heart Institute at New York Presbyterian/Columbia Medical Center. Above all, he appears to be a wonderfully caring individual with an open and personable nature. As you listen to Dr. Oz, you are immediately drawn in. Watching him, you see a consummate celebrity who is curious, understanding, and reverent. You marvel at his accomplishment, but you see power in his compassion, receptivity, and partnership with those around him. Dr. Oz speaks to our concerns and inspires us to be a part of his experiences.

Peter's Engagement Challenge

Our case study Peter has three interesting engagement challenges. As plant manager of a newly acquired facility, Peter is expected to quickly integrate his plant into the greater organization. He is also expected to develop relationships with the plant's two primary customers in Asia, in ethnic cultural groups with whom he has had little experience. Lastly, Peter is expected to develop better collaborative relationships with his current, diverse peer group.

Peter is a straightforward leader. He plans and executes well. He is fair, but tough minded. Looking at Peter in relation to the specific traits of engaging leadership, we would find Peter not typically *inquisitive* by nature. He tends to focus on what is in front of him, rather than being spurred to probe farther, especially into the thoughts of others. That said, his skill at *listening* with attention and for accurate understanding is still above average. His politeness conveys a highly *respectful* tone. He would also be viewed as *responsive.* If an issue or concern is raised he addresses it. He believes in the power of teamwork and works hard at being *inclusive,* drawing everyone on his immediate team in. He gives responsibility to others, *empowering* them to develop their own skills. He does not, however, translate his *collaborative* skill at working along with others to how he works with his current peer group.

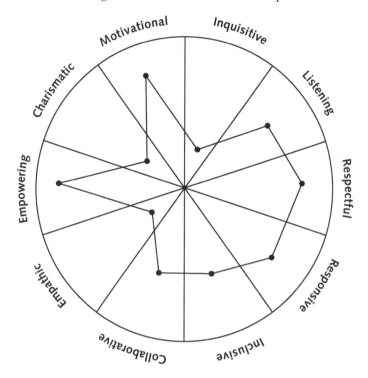

Figure 3.4 Peter's Ratings for Traits of ENGAGING Leadership

Additionally, Peter does not identify well with perspectives outside of his own. He is not *empathic*. He works best in homogeneous environments. Peter is *motivational* in that he makes it a leadership practice to recognize others' accomplishments both formally and informally. Yet, he lacks the *charismatic* enthusiasm that can inspire others by sheer force of presence. Peter's engaging leadership ratings are seen in Figure 3.4.

Peter's high scores on *respectful, responsive,* and *empowering,* along with high-average scores on *listening* and *motivational* provide a solid foundation for engagement. His scores on *collaborative* and *inclusive* are in the moderate range because, while he is collaborative and inclusive within teams he has direct responsibility for, he does not work in a shared manner across the greater organization, for example, with his current peer group. His low score on *charismatic* is not so much a concern as he is looked up to nonetheless. The areas Peter needs to address are his low scores on *inquisitive* and *empathic*. Peter needs these traits to build partnerships with his two key customer groups and to relate better to his peers.

Journaling for Discovery

Looking at Peter's primary areas of concern, inquisitiveness and empathy, how can Peter build skill in these traits of engaging leadership? In particular, can he develop a curiosity about, an understanding of, and appreciation for his customers and peers? Peter can begin to address both skill needs with the help of journaling, a writing tool that can take many forms, from the structured to the unstructured. Logs and diaries are more structured forms of journaling. Here, the unstructured form will be called a journal with the structured form referred to as logging.

Peter could journal about observations and insights as they come to him. Journal entries can be expressed in words or pictures or a combination of the two. The journaling that Peter would do will require a shift in style from his usual organized, disciplined mode to him becoming more of an explorer, someone heading out in the world to discover new insights and information. The subject of Peter's exploration would be cultural diversity, exploring various aspects of cultures different from his own.

Peter's cultural experiences are limited, and to date his assignments have based him at his work locations dealing with those on his geographic team. He is now expected to work in a broader way across the greater organization and to interact more directly with customers. Peter has little or no experience with the cultures of his key customers or of the cultures of several members of his peer group. Peter should keep his cultural journal with him at all times for six months to record his thoughts and observations on anything he encounters concerning culture that is new, odd, rare, or different. He can ask questions about what he observes and record the answers. He should suspend judgment or evaluation; in this activity he is a neutral, inquisitive observer on a discovery mission. During this process, Peter should periodically reflect on his journal's contents and write anything that comes to mind about how what he has learned can facilitate favorable interactions with his customers and peers.

To further support Peter in developing broader empathy and sensitize him to the perspectives of others, Peter can also use a tangible cue. Peter has a six-year-old son named Daniel with whom Peter is very close. Peter's wife had Daniel's first pair of shoes bronzed a few years ago. She keeps one on her desk at work and Peter keeps one on his. Peter could use Daniel's shoe to cue him to think of the perspective of others. The metaphor for empathy is to walk in the shoes of another. Peter can use Daniel as his inspiration in his journey to become more empathic.

Becoming Empathic

Empathy is an ability to understand and identify with another's perspective. To identify with someone else is not an intellectual understanding of content, but it is an appreciation of their view, and more importantly, the feelings and perceptions that drive that view. Often, in trying to influence others we are focused on presenting our view, on selling our point. It is difficult, if not impossible, to tune in to those around us when we are focused on ourselves. Empathy turns the focus toward others in order to get a good read on their thoughts, beliefs, feelings, and needs.

Can empathy be learned or is it a preference, an innate ability that some of us have and some do not? Peter has been given a plan to learn to be more empathic. The implication is that he can learn to do so. The fact is we can learn this potent skill. It is a matter of belief that there is value in doing so. It is a matter of will to turn the focus over to others. It is a matter of discipline, structuring opportunities to practice empathy over and over again. To support Peter's empathic development he can learn and practice active listening. Peter is a good factual listener. He listens for relevant details, but is he an active listener? Can he listen for meaning, perceptions, and experiences?

Active Listening and Behavior Rehearsal

The key element of empathy is active listening, which has three components: attending, paraphrasing, and validating.[20] You attend to what the other person is saying, not just to the words or the topic but to the nature of the experience. What does the other person feel? What meaning does the situation have for him or her? You paraphrase back what you heard. You don't parrot the other's words, but in your own words capture the essence of his or her experience. It is important to get to the level of that experience—not the facts of the situation but the real meaning. Validation is a gut check with the other person. Give him or her the chance to tell you how close or far off you are and to provide more information if necessary.

The most difficult part in mastering empathy, for many, is in slowing your own forward momentum. To take the time to shift focus from your sales pitch to understanding where the other person is coming from seems not just a waste of time, but like backtracking. In fact, taking the time to become a more empathic leader will plant many seeds for future buy-in, it will give you important insights into your people, and it will keep you from being blindsided. Consider this example.

Non-Empathic Approach

A company regional president calls in one of her directors and makes a strong case for why this new vendor has to be handled a certain way. She gives her director all of the facts and data, states emphatically how important this transition is to the company CEO, and asks her director if he has any questions. The director asks a few peripheral questions and looks obviously concerned, but he doesn't verbalize anything. The president asks if she can count on the director to make this happen. He says yes and leaves.

Empathic Approach

The same president calls her person in, runs down the situation, notes her director's concern, and makes a comment before the director leaves the room.

President: You seem disturbed about something.

Director: No, but I am worried. There's a lot of grumbling in the organization right now.

President: What concerns you most about what you are hearing?

Director: I guess it's just one more example of the unrest in the organization.

President: So, this isn't about this new vendor policy specifically, but about a bigger problem in how the team is faring?

Director: Yes, in particular, that there have been many changes and little if any communication about where this is all headed. I seem to be spending a lot of time dealing with conflicts and pushback that didn't typically occur before. I can deal with it; I just think it is unnecessary and frankly a waste of energy. I want to be able to push the group harder now more than ever, and I don't see that they can rise to the occasion under the current conditions.

President: You mean the perceived secrecy, like something more is going to happen?

Director: That's a good way to put it.

What do you notice about the difference in these two dialogues? In the first dialogue, the president makes a request, sells her point, and gets verbal compliance. In the second dialogue, the president makes a request, sells her point, and gains a perspective about potential trouble ahead. She brings her director into the leadership equation and enters into a collaboration based on empathy with her director's present experience. The empathic president listened and captured an accurate understanding of the nature of the director's concern. Disciplining yourself to practice empathy during each key dialogue will begin to make the practice second nature. Practicing a new skill over and over is known as behavior rehearsal. You repeat the new behavior until it becomes second nature. Empathy is a valuable leadership tool that can be learned and in Peter's case is a depth development opportunity worth exploring further. As Peter works to develop his engaging traits using unstructured journaling, cuing, and active listening, he will be developing greater right brain breadth as well, shifting style from structured to unstructured and from the known to the new. In particular, journaling will help Peter shift style further from his **methodical** preferences to the **innovative** traits *novelty seeking, experimental,* and *curious*. Active listening will help him to become more intuitive.

Peter's ENGAGING Style Shift Summary

High scores: *Listening, respectful, responsive, empowering, motivational*

Alter-brain depth targets: *Inquisitive, empathic* (Note that difficulties with *inclusive* and *collaborative* are situational and thought to improve with improvement in inquisitive and empathic traits)

Tools: Journaling, cuing, active listening, behavior rehearsal, SME Goleman to better understand empathy

Alter-brain breadth impact: Journaling and active listening will help shift Peter's left brain **methodical** mindset to the right brain behaviors **strategic** (trait *intuitive*) and **innovative** (traits *novelty-seeking, experimental, curious*)

Much has been conveyed about the behavior **engaging**. In closing this section, the following assessment is offered to assist you in determining your own inclinations in this area.

How Engaging Are You?

The following questions will give you something to think about:

1. Do you motivate others regularly through praise and rewards?
2. Do you really listen—not just hear, but listen?
3. Do you seek input?
4. Do you solicit input from those less likely to speak up?
5. Do you know everyone on your extended team?
6. Do you seek inclusion or play favorites?
7. Can you see things from others' perspectives, or is it hard to get out of your own mindset?
8. Are you nice?
9. Do you treat others with respect?
10. Do you delegate?
11. Do you let others do it their way?

12. Do you turn over the power when it is appropriate?
13. Do you address others' concerns?
14. Are you curious?
15. How compelling are you?

Nonverbal Behavior and Engagement

The communication rule of thumb is that upwards of seventy percent of our communication is nonverbal. That means others pay less attention to what we say and more attention to how we say it. Aspects of nonverbal communication include facial expressions, eye contact, touch, gestures, silence, voice tone, rate of speech, laughter, yelling, whining, and pitch.[21]

Nonverbal communication is a critical factor in engagement. Your nonverbal behavior will ultimately be what communicates your messages to those you are trying to influence. Consider just one aspect of nonverbal communication, your tone of voice. Whether you are trying to praise someone, deliver a tough message about their performance, sway them, or get them to buy in to a new way of looking at something, your tone can and will determine the outcome.

Think of a difficult message you have to convey to someone, such as "George, your performance is dropping off because you are not involving Ann in the projects." Try saying the same message aloud two different ways. First, say it with impatience and frustration. Next, say it in a calm yet firm way with a steady voice. Try the same exercise with something positive. "Ed, you did a great job." First, say it with heartfelt enthusiasm. Next, say it without emotion, matter-of-fact-like. Tone is one powerful nonverbal engager. If you want to enhance your ability to engage others, pay close attention to your nonverbal cues—facial expressions, voice tone, gestures, and eye contact. Doing so will make you a better overall engaging leader.

Visioning for Right Brain Inspiration

Just as Peter came up with his son's shoe as an inspiration for developing empathy, I would like you to create your own inspiration for right brain leadership. In ending this chapter, join in an activity. What you will do is close your eyes and take a slow, deep breath. Think for a moment about the knowledge you now have about being **strategic, innovative, transformational**, and **engaging**—the behaviors of your Line of SITE. How can this knowledge at this moment in time help take you and your team to the next level? Stop and imagine that it is six months from now, and you are leading with greater breadth and depth in right brain leadership ability. Visualize what that looks like. How are you interacting with your people? How are they responding to you? You are in the midst of a visioning activity. Visioning is both a fundamental leadership process and a valuable right brain leadership tool—to think about how you want things to be, to imagine with specific detail and clarity. Now open your eyes and draw an image or write down a phrase to capture the essence of your thinking. This is your inspiration for right brain leadership.

CHAPTER 4

LEFT BRAIN LEADERSHIP: THE MEGA MIND

Never neglect details. When everyone's mind is dulled or distracted the leader must be doubly vigilant.

—*Colin Powell*

I have a colleague who worked on the staff of two of our nation's presidents. We were having dinner one night talking about his experiences. Curiosity got the best of me. I asked what a typical day was like at the White House. He said that he arrived at work around 5:00 a.m. greeted by his staff, who briefed him on anything and everything relevant to the coming day. Pressing issues were flagged, and matters requiring immediate action were addressed. Concurrently, a cadre of workers sorted through demands, set priorities, and scoped out the day with minute-by-minute precision. The details he and his team managed on any given day and the exhaustive protocols to be followed required the utmost in planning, communication, stewardship, and execution. In an environment like the White House, flawless *looking over* is the expected, the epitome of the **MEGA Mind** in action.

While most of us do not face the demands of the White House, we all tend to our own scope of responsibilities. The MEGA Mind enables us to see our tasks with clarity and work toward our ultimate goals. The MEGA Mind contributes to our ongoing effectiveness in dealing with the work at hand. It is a factor in how well we communicate and are able to provide stability. The MEGA Mind also speaks to our ability to drive for results. This chapter will examine the four behaviors of the MEGA Mind, along with each behavior's corresponding traits. The four behaviors of the MEGA Mind as defined are:

Methodical: to plan well; to be systematic and effectual in your approach to initiatives

Expressive: to clearly communicate your thoughts both formally and informally while providing the necessary context

Grounded: to act with integrity, consistency, and stability; to be the steward and the gauge

Assertive: to be upfront, direct, and determined in order to get the desired results

METHODICAL

> A goal without a plan is just a wish.
>
> —*Antoine de Saint-Exupery*

The plan that continues to impress me is the one responsible for landing men on the moon and returning them safely. Think about the details that went into such an endeavor. The leadership behavior **methodical** requires that you plan well, taking into consideration all tasks and details. It also means that you are efficient and systematic in your approach. Being methodical means that you employ scrutiny to come to solid conclusions. The ten traits of **METHODICAL** leadership are:

Task oriented – being attentive to assignments

Detail oriented – being attentive to the discrete parts of assignments

Organized – being orderly and systematic

Effective – producing workable solutions or results

Focused – able to establish and attend to priorities

Procedural – using systems and processes

Sequential – being cognizant of the likely order of things

Logical – being rational and reasonable, recognizing what makes the best sense

Analytical – breaking an entity into its parts

Factual – basing assertions on tangible data and evidence

Methodical is the first leadership behavior of the MEGA Mind, because planning is primal to left brain leadership success. In a definitive shift from the right brain strategist, the methodical leader is all about present realities.

The Checklist

If you were to examine your current methodical approach, what would you note? Where are your strengths and gaps? Below are the ten traits of methodical leadership as a checklist. A checklist is a commonly used planning tool. Think of how you typically approach your work. Go down the checklist and rate yourself from zero (0) to ten (10) with ten being the high score and see how you fare. Answer for yourself the question: how well do I measure up to the expectation contained in each definition?

Methodical Leadership Checklist

___ **Task oriented:** ground my day in the assignments at hand

___ **Detail oriented:** ground my day in the discrete parts of the assignments

___ **Organized:** consider how to resource and track the work to ensure systematic order

___ **Effective:** consider the conditions that would need to be met in order to meet goals in the best way possible, netting workable solutions or results

___ **Focused:** examine the work scope and resources available in order to prioritize tasks and initiatives and attend to those established

___ **Procedural:** ensure that adequate processes and systems are in place

___ **Sequential:** determine the best order and time frames for the work

___ **Logical:** look back over the plan to date to ensure that it makes good overall sense

___ **Analytical:** examine elements and relationships for plan and goal strengths, weaknesses, opportunities, and threats

___ **Factual:** provide the facts to back up assertions

I asked one of my clients to complete the checklist based on his current day-to-day work practices. He is a senior engineer and through both his inherent personality and engineering training, he is what most would consider highly methodical. But he has struggled lately. He reported that his organization is in reactive mode and that he tends to go where the crisis leads him. He also said that the sheer volume of the work makes prioritizing difficult, if not impossible. For this engineer, use of the methodical trait checklist helped him identify where and how he had drifted off course. Checklists provide a left brain discipline that can help us override chaos around us. Our engineer has a preference for structure, but his environment made it difficult for him to follow his preference. If you are not so naturally disposed, a checklist can help you shift style in a more structured direction. A checklist is a simple, straightforward, left brain tool.

Can Madison Make the Left Brain Shift?

Madison was discussed as a high-energy, creative leader who is a great match for the company's high-energy, creative culture. However, the growth of the business and demands of the marketplace have left the organization frenetic. Madison is seen as a solid innovative leader but as one who also needs to be able to ground her team to meet the current business demands. Madison's difficulties with respect to structure, in particular her ability to drive focus, have been flagged as a development need. When we left off in Chapter 3, she had brainstormed ways to address her problem with focus. She came up with many interesting ideas. Now it is time for her to shift style and address not only her focus but to look at her methodical leadership ability overall. Using our circle chart, Madison's ratings for the ten traits of methodical leadership are shown in Figure 4.1.

When broken down trait by trait, Madison has three methodical strong suits. Her score on *effective* shows that she knows what right looks like and what would constitute a desired means and result. Her thinking ability is *logical*. She is rational and reasonable. She has good common sense. She also is *analytical*, breaking constructs down into parts and examining problems and issues piece by piece. Madison's methodical weaknesses, however, far outweigh her strengths. Seven traits in total, her gaps are in the areas of being *task* and *detail oriented*, *organized*,

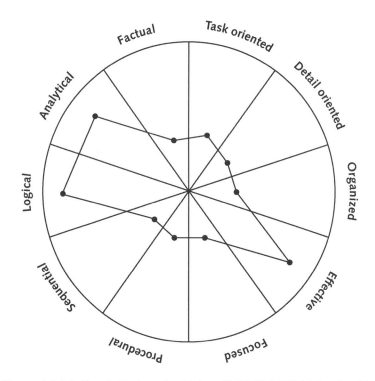

Figure 4.1 Madison's Ratings for Traits of METHODICAL Leadership

focused, sequential, factual, and *procedural.* While she likes to examine the elements of a problem, she is less disposed to give attention to the discrete parts of assignments. Her innovative inclinations seem at odds with order, systems, and processes. She also allows the attention to shift from one task to another without identifying and holding to established priorities. Additionally, Madison needs to develop a greater appreciation for tangible data and evidence to complement her more intuitive sense. In all, Madison needs to develop discipline in identifying the scope of the work and in setting and tracking priorities, develop facility with supportive processes, and develop systems and applications for the use of quantifiable information.

In assessing Madison's methodical leadership in this way, we see that her development needs are broader than learning how to focus better. She needs to develop seven of ten aspects of methodical leadership. Knowing what we know about Madison, about her preference for divergent thought, getting her grounded in *what is* and not being wooed away by *what could be* is the nature of the challenge. She also needs to shift style from the strategic trait *conceptual* to the methodical trait *factual.* The fact that she possesses some methodical skill, that she is able to be effective, logical, and analytical, shows ability once the order is imposed. However, Madison needs to be the one imposing the order and using her existing methodical strengths to help her along the way. Madison needs assistance developing traits that enable her to get her arms around and remain in day-to-day control of the work scope and its related parts. She also needs to seek out and rely more on hard data to inform her thinking and decision making, to be more factual. Using quantitative measures to assess and gauge progress is new to her and a practice she needs to add to how she looks over the work. This will make her more factual, dealing with precise and actual realities.

Madison needs to rely on basic left brain tools, such as checklists and planning aids. Fortunately for Madison, multiple technologies that organize, prompt, and display the work are available. These range from simple year-at-a-glance calendars to more complex computer software programs. She needs to use these aids to plan out and track the work days, weeks, and months ahead in a way that ensures all assignments are fully managed. For Madison, this is simply a discipline she is going to have to train herself in and hold herself to through constant behavior rehearsal.

Madison's Dynamic Interplay

If Madison accepts the challenge to develop her methodical skills and add them to her innovative and strategic strengths, she will possess a powerful combination. She will be poised to lead with a dynamic interplay between the right brain **strategic** and **innovative** and the left brain

methodical. Shifting style between methodical control of the work and innovative execution, she will lead her team to substantive project outcomes. The outcomes that she and her team produce will have maximum impact for the business.

But how will she make this shift? How can she move from the conceptual to the factual? Two tools can help her shift style. The first tool is the mind mapping explained in Chapter 3. Mind mapping has applications for both creating and planning.[1] Just as Madison used brainstorming to help her focus, she can use this imaginative tool to help her shift style to the left brain. Madison could mind map a plan to seek out, utilize, and rely on factual data. The second tool is a data log. Madison could develop a data log that tracks her use of factual and conceptual data. The log could be set up to enter factual data on one page and conceptual data on the page opposite it. Capturing the data side by side would give Madison a visual reference for how balanced her data access is. Being an artist, visual references are easy for her to relate to.

The Priorities Battle

Given the sheer volume of work we face today, setting and keeping to the correct priorities is a complex challenge. Madison has difficulty with focus, and prioritizing is a key aspect of focus. The brainstorm activity she completed in Chapter 3 was meant to help her begin to focus better. Changing priorities seem to be more and more the rule rather than the exception these days and, as such, will continue to present focus trials for leaders. In tracking leadership struggles over the past five years, changing priorities comes up over and over again as a primary distraction. Organizations seem to have fairly stable processes for setting priorities through strategic and operations planning processes. Then the fun begins. Opportunities appear, clients demand change, internal problems occur, leaders change, and the priority battle is in full swing. A clearly defined process for changing priorities is rarely if ever in place. It often comes down to a "because I said so" message from the leader with the most power. The ripple effects are rampant.

There is no simple fix for the priority struggles you face. This issue is introduced here at the end of the section on methodical leadership to make the point that priority setting is a complex iterative process involving all aspects of methodical leadership, not just focus. A change in priorities, while inevitable, needs to occur in a better framework than currently exists today. The optimal framework would draw upon both left brain logic and order and right brain holistics. As we move through the remaining behaviors, think of what happens in your organization relative to priority shifting. What behaviors and traits could you draw from to ease those changes, making them less jarring to all concerned? At times you yourself will be instigating the changes; at other times those above you will be calling for them. How can and will you react?

In Madison's case, she first needs to land on the successful use of fundamental methodical skills, to be more task and detail oriented, more organized, focused, sequential, and procedural. She then needs to develop her use of factual data and work on her style shift between the factual and the conceptual. Having better depth in methodical ability and being able to attain a dynamic interplay from the methodical to the strategic will then put her in a position to begin to better address the quagmire of priority shifts. Madison has a long way to go in establishing herself in this way, but once she does her impact will increase exponentially.

Madison's METHODICAL Style Shift Summary

High scores: *Effective, logical, analytical*

Alter-brain depth targets: *Task* and *detail oriented, organized, focused, sequential, procedural, factual*

Tools: Checklists, mind mapping, planning aids

Alter-brain breadth target: To shift style from **strategic** (trait *conceptual*) to **methodical** (trait *factual*) and work to create a balanced dynamic interplay between the two

---

Methodical leadership ensures that through sound planning you will effectively manage ongoing demands. What comes to mind next is the importance of communication to both the development and tracking of those plans. The second behavior of the MEGA Mind is **expressive**.

EXPRESSIVE

> The character of a man is known from his conversations.
>
> —*Menander*

The place was New York City. The date was July 12, 1976. The event was the Democratic National Convention. The speaker was Barbara Jordan, an African American pioneer in the U.S. House of Representatives. Her opening statement was compelling, direct, and powerful as only Jordan could be: "There is something special about tonight. What is the difference? What is special? I, Barbara Jordan, am a keynote speaker...And I feel notwithstanding the past, my presence here is one additional bit of evidence that the American Dream need not forever be deferred."[2] Jordan's full address that evening was noted as one of the most compelling in the convention's history. Through her commanding expressive ability, her striking character was revealed. Jordan's sense of presence and her exuberant words displayed her patriotism, loyalty, and duty to her country. She also showed us her belief in dreams being realized, that we could and should all aspire to greatness. Her strength of conviction and her civic duty and pride, all parts of her character, were apparent in what she said and how she said it.

The leadership behavior **expressive** relates to being able to clearly communicate your thoughts. It means that you provide audiences with the needed context, that you converse and come across well, and that you are compelling and encouraging. Being expressive means that you can master all mediums, from face-to-face conversations to formal presentations, e-mail, conference calls, and written memos and doctrine. To be expressive is to ensure that information, messages, and mandates are well articulated. The traits of **EXPRESSIVE** leadership are:

Prepared – giving the necessary forethought to formal and informal messages

Articulate – able to write or speak with clarity

Coherent – able to write or speak logically

Concise – able to write or speak succinctly

Erudite – able to express yourself from the basis of scholarly knowledge

Presentable – having a professional presence and appearance

Passionate – having intensity and/or enthusiasm with respect to your subject matter

Personable – having an appropriately favorable demeanor

Persuasive – able to make a compelling point

Interesting – provoking thought and/or holding others' attention

Expressive Mechanics and Persona

If asked to create a "state of the business" elevator speech to deliver at your next staff meeting using as many of the above traits as possible, what would your message be? Case study Angela is considered a solid expressive leader. Her elevator speech to her team follows:

> Okay everyone, we are at midyear and I want to tell you where we stand. Our numbers are solid, not great, but on target. Industry projections tell us that the second half will be challenging in that a portion of our bread and butter sales are going to drop by twenty percent due to rising interest rates. Those of us who have been here for a while may recall that we were in a similar situation five years back when we lost two key customers midyear, and we were able to recover with a great result. We pulled together and

came up with some pretty creative solutions. There's no reason why we can't do that again. If anything, we are a stronger team now. Let's push ourselves and see what we come up with. I'm going to be holding a series of brainstorming sessions with small groups. Everyone in this room will be included. You may be surprised at how the groups are arranged, but I believe that if we get some different people together, we'll get some different results, don't you? Pre-questions will be posted tomorrow for the group sessions, so you'll have time to do some advance thinking. I look forward to the second half of the year and to great results.

How do you think Angela did? When evaluating someone's expressive ability, it does not take long to come to the realization that expressiveness has two sides to it. One side reflects the more technical aspects of communicating, what you say. Communication is also about your delivery, how you say it along with other qualities like your appearance. Think of the ten traits of expressiveness as being organized into the *mechanics* of expression and your expressive *persona*. Being prepared, articulate, coherent, concise, and erudite are all mechanics of communicating. Being presentable, passionate, personable, persuasive, and interesting reflect your expressive persona. Angela's ratings broken down by persona and mechanics are shown in Figure 4.2.

Angela's speech to her team demonstrated several expressive strengths. She was **articulate**. She expressed herself clearly. She was **concise**, speaking to the point as she always does. She is not one to ramble or make long protracted points. If we could see and hear her, we would note that she was **presentable**, appropriately reflecting her executive position. Angela was **personable**. She was pleasant and welcoming. She typically speaks with a tone that others find easy to listen to. She also was **passionate** in her conviction. Angela was able to make compelling points and as such was **persuasive**.

Angela could have enhanced her impact by being more **prepared**, **coherent, erudite**, and **interesting**. Backing up her key messages with examples of noteworthy company, customer, or marketplace data would have enhanced her preparedness. Being better prepared is sometimes a matter of advance researching of facts that support your key messages. Being better prepared may also come from having exposure to dynamic speaking models like Barbara Jordan. Angela should seek out opportunities to view expert speakers to see what she can learn from their style and approaches.

Angela attempted to bring interest into her speech by introducing a story. In that story, she reflected on the past, but it was not really interesting. It did not capture the audience's attention to the extent that it could have. Story-telling is a well-received adjunct to any talk or speech, especially when others can relate firsthand to the characters in the story. Taking

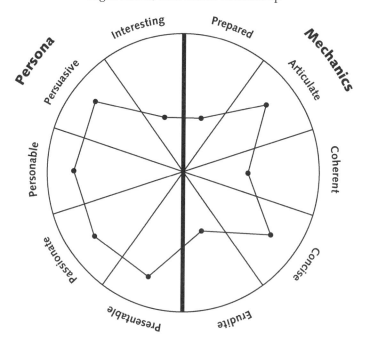

Figure 4.2 Angela's Ratings for Traits of EXPRESSIVE Leadership Grouped by Persona and Mechanics

her story-telling further would add interest and nicely complement Angela's expressive effectiveness. Story-telling is an art that she may want to consider studying more formally through a workshop or seminar. Being more interesting could also be accomplished by Angela leveraging her natural enthusiasm. She tends to come across as professional to a fault when presenting or speaking formally. She should use her natural warmth and charm to her benefit in both formal and informal settings.

As a final aspect of the trait *interesting*, while Angela is a solid conventional speaker, she could take her presentations to the next level by preparing differently. By adding an element of the innovative—imaginative—she would capture her audience more fully. This style shift to the innovative could also serve to break her out of her habitual ways in a manner that is enhancing, yet still true to who she is. It may also help her jolt her team in a non-confrontational way into a more receptive frame of mind.

Erudition is an inclination of Angela's that she tends to play down. Shifting style to her transformational strong suit, *open to learning*, to draw on her diverse knowledge base by sharing inspirational facts, quotes, or perspectives would serve her well when speaking.

Coherence is about writing or speaking logically, your argument or position being compelling because it makes good sense. Angela's state of the business speech attempted to compel using persuasion and passion, not reason. She appealed to her audience through her relationship with them. She did not necessarily walk them through a logical set of points or a business rationale for change. Given her current circumstance, that her team is resisting change, Angela needed to better leverage a coherent argument. Doing so would have communicated a definitive message to the group that change was both necessary and inevitable.

Overall, she showed great depth in expressive persona with one area of persona to enhance, being more interesting. Angela showed competency in expressive mechanics but had three areas to work on: being prepared, coherent, and erudite.

Angela's EXPRESSIVE Style Shift Summary

High scores: *Articulate, concise, presentable, personable, persuasive, passionate*

Alter-brain depth targets: *Prepared, erudite, coherent, interesting*

Tools: Planning aids, SME assistance in developing story-telling ability and dynamic speaking, use own diverse knowledge base

Alter-brain breadth target: To complement expressive ability with style shifts to **innovative** (traits *playful, curious, imaginative*—new qualities for her) and to **transformational** (trait *open to learning*—something she is already adept at)

Communication 101

Unlike Angela, some leaders struggle with communication. Some leaders over-communicate, while other leaders need to step up and speak out. Expressiveness is an interesting behavior to attempt to modify in either direction. Sometimes simply noting common pitfalls helps direct improvement. Here are ten common expressive pitfalls to think about and avoid.

1. Repeating yourself. Be mindful of what you say and when you say it. If you are going to repeat yourself, declare it and do it for a reason. Say, "I know I said this at the last staff meeting, but I am going to say it again because..." and then tell them why you need to reiterate.

2. Talking too much. If you talk too much you will get negative fallout. Some will tune you out, others will feel oppressed, and still others will feel compelled to challenge you, just for the sake of having their say. More is definitely not better when it comes to expressiveness.

3. Talking too little. Just as some leaders talk too much, others talk too little. You need to speak to your people. Tell them what they need to know, tell them

what you think, and tell them what you expect. The strong silent type is for the cinema, not for leadership.

4. Thinking that talking is persuading. Persuasiveness is about what you say and how you say it, not about how much you say.

5. Communicating only in your comfortable style. Communicate with your audience in mind. What you are comfortable with may not be appropriate for every audience. When in doubt, a middle of the road, clear and concise approach is the best.

6. Giving opinions. Opinions are a powerful leadership tool. They should be used wisely. Some of us are more opinionated than others. Opinions should not be expressed or withheld as part of a personality style, but rather as a conscious communication strategy.

7. Going for broke. Don't try to get everything said on one slide, during one presentation, in one phone call, or at one meeting. Plant seeds which you go back and reinforce along the way, or hit key highlights. Say to yourself, "What are the one, two, or three things I want them to leave here remembering?" Then note where you have to go back and cultivate the seedlings.

8. Focusing on your words and not on your actions. This point, raised previously in Chapter 3 under the section on engaging leadership, is important enough to warrant being repeated. The communication rule of thumb is that upwards of seventy percent of our communication is nonverbal. That means others pay less attention to what we say and more attention to how we say it. Pay attention to your nonverbal cues—facial expressions, voice tone, gestures, and eye contact, to name a few—and give nonverbal communication the attention it deserves.

9. Thinking you need to shake them up. You need to inspire, not paralyze. Focus on what you can say to spur others forward rather than freeze them in their tracks. Always think of promoting forward motion.

10. Work is serious business. It is, but a little fun never hurt. Lighter voice tones and levity can add to your expressive power and help get those around you to be more productive.

In order to avoid many of the common pitfalls of expressive leadership, you should think in terms of how others feel in your presence. Consider how grounded you are.

GROUNDED

> Nearly all men can stand adversity, but if you want to test his character,
> give him power.
>
> —*Abraham Lincoln*

Leaders have power. How they handle that power will determine, among other things, how grounded a leader they are. In Lincoln's terms, how one handles power will reflect one's character. The leadership behavior **grounded** is defined as acting with integrity, consistency, and stability, to be the steward and the gauge. It is about how others feel in your presence. If you are a grounded leader, others will feel as though they are in good hands. Others also will see you as possessing a favorable character.

Taking the High Road

When I think of power and character as correlated to grounded leadership, one contemporary leader comes to mind. As vice president of the United States, Al Gore was at the height of his professional career and at the height of his power. He then ran for the presidency and faced his darkest professional moment. His power was abruptly taken away. Here we saw not only how a leader acted with power but also how a leader acted when his power circumstance dramatically changed. When Gore lost the 2000 presidential election to George W. Bush under controversial circumstances, he could have reacted in a number of ways. Gore chose to take the high road. He regrouped and focused his energies on the greater good. Gore now leads an international awareness and action campaign against the threat of global warming. He lectures internationally, has produced an award-winning documentary, and promotes clear and simple ways through which we all can make a difference. For this work, Gore was the 2007 recipient of a Nobel Prize. In both how he handled his rise to and fall from power and how he leads his latest initiative, we see exemplary character and exemplary use of power. We see grounded leadership.

Looking more closely at what it means to be grounded, the ten traits of **GROUNDED** leadership are:

Composed – able to control your emotions

Approachable – having a manner that allows others to reach out to you

Genuine – being sincere

Pragmatic – being practical and realistic

Cautious – being sensible and careful

Questioning – seeking assurances and/or getting to the bottom of issues

Stable – being steady and consistent in your views and approaches

Loyal – being committed to your people and responsibilities

Established – having proven competence

Trustworthy – able to be counted on

Relating the ten traits of grounded leadership to Gore, we see a leader who is generally composed. He appears approachable and easy to talk to. He also appears genuine in wanting to make a difference. His actions relative to environmental reform are pragmatic. Gore's platform presents cautious rather than rash solutions, and he is questioning in a way that provokes our own thinking. Gore has a reputation for being stable, loyal, and established as well as trustworthy; although for him and for all leaders, trust is something to be earned time and time again as roles evolve and challenges are taken on.

The ten traits of grounded leadership can be organized into three clusters. The first cluster represents *initial impressions*, how others experience a leader in the moment. How composed, approachable, and genuine is she? The second cluster represents a leader's grounded *actions*, how a leader responds to a given situation. Is he practical? Does she exercise good caution? Does he or she ask the right questions? The third cluster reflects a leader's *reputation* over time. How steady, loyal, and established is he? Can we trust him to deliver on his promises?

Ken's Grounded Approach

While not a famous public figure, our case study Ken has several grounded leadership strengths. Those strengths lie in the cluster for actions. Ken is **pragmatic** and highly **cautious**. He is exceedingly practical and always careful to find the more sensible solutions. Ken is good at getting to the bottom of issues through a style that reflects sound **questioning**. Ken is less adept when it comes to initial impressions. He is not **composed** when challenged and often prone to outbursts. Ken is seen as less than **approachable**, and many are not comfortable talking with him. Others see him as driving his own agenda and not **genuine** or sincere in his encouragement to them. With respect to Ken's reputation he also has difficulty. While he is given credit for being **established**, or competent, he is not seen as **stable, loyal,** or **trustworthy.** Others experience Ken as inconsistent and out for himself.

Ken is a driver, and like many drivers, he often negates the importance of in-the-moment impressions. Ken is future focused, and the present is of less concern for him. To compound Ken's situation, during stressful times he comes across as unnerved and unapproachable. Ken is not concerned with what is happening in front of him. He is busy driving for where he wants to be. When he struggles to get there, he reacts negatively.

What Ken and other drivers like him need to understand is that initial impressions set a powerful tone. Initial impressions are not the same as first impressions; rather, initial impressions are how one is experienced each time an interaction is initiated with someone. Poor initial impressions can impact one's reputation. While Ken is accomplished and his intentions are good, his people do not see him as stable and loyal, someone they can trust. They do not view him as having the better reputation he may deserve. His initial impressions taint his reputation.

It is unlikely that a leader's reputation will be favorable if initial impressions are negative. Social intelligence theory tells us that. People need to experience favorable social cues in order to have favorable impressions. Grounded leadership is not about what a leader has accomplished but about how others experience his accomplishment. Figure 4.3 shows Ken's ratings for the traits of grounded leadership, organized by initial impressions, actions, and reputation.

Breathe

How can Ken come across better? How can he become more composed, approachable, and genuine? How can he begin to improve his reputation? One tool to help Ken is breathing—not the kind of breathing that we do automatically, but deep breathing. Deep breathing is the foundation of many, if not all, relaxation exercises, and of yoga and meditation. Many of these experiences contain four basic elements: a quiet setting, something to concentrate on, a passive mindset, and a comfortable position.[3]

Deep breathing has long been found to help reduce stress, improving thought clarity. Many believe it facilitates overall health and well-being.[4]

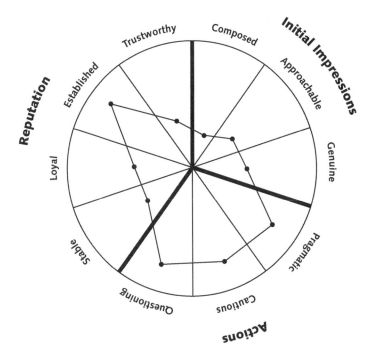

Figure 4.3 Ken's Ratings for Traits of GROUNDED Leadership Grouped by Cluster

Ken's driven nature makes it difficult for him to be composed in the present. For him, the experience of the present is usually unfavorable. In the present, Ken immediately focuses on what he is not happy with or where he wants to get. He is often frustrated by the fact that he is not there yet. Ken needs to slow his mind and body down and be more comfortable in and focused on the present. One way for Ken to slow down is through deep breathing.

To be most helpful, deep breathing should be done several times a day at regular intervals. You can also practice deep breathing before going into a stressful meeting, to help you fall asleep, before turning on the car to go to and come from work, in airports or on airplanes. Practice deep breathing anywhere you need to take a break, calm down, or in Ken's case, slow down.

There are several techniques for deep breathing. The process presented here is a simple form that can be done anywhere you can find a quiet place to sit. Close your eyes, seat yourself comfortably, rest your arms on your legs and take slow deep breaths, the kind that fill your abdomen rather than contract it. Deep breathing takes practice. You need to build up to a true, slow, deep breath. You accomplish that by focusing on your breathing speed and progressively increasing breathing depth. At first take slow, shallow breaths. Deepen the breaths as you go along. While you are breathing, clear your mind of distractions. To help, focus your attention on a prompting phrase, one that will, in essence, tell your brain to respond differently than it has in the past. In Ken's case, he would have previously entered into an interaction saying something to himself along the lines of "Why am I here? This is a huge waste of my time." This time he will use the phrase "right here, right now" to cue himself that coming across better in the moment is important to his success. He will continue to breath and resist distractions using his prompting phrase, "right here, right now." When he is ready, he will initiate an interaction that is calmer from the breathing and focused from the prompting phrase. Deep breathing can give Ken the benefit he needs in just a few minutes. A few deep breaths will slow Ken down and enable him to come across better. He will feel calmer even in the face of stress, and once calm, he can begin to convey better initial impressions.

Developing greater approachability and genuineness as well as being seen as more stable, loyal, and trustworthy can be aided by Ken making a style shift to the behavior **engaging**. Ken is currently seen as driving his own agenda and as being out for himself. He is not someone others feel comfortable holding conversations with. To be engaging is to understand and work well with others, to validate, involve, and recognize others, and to help them take on responsibility. Ken is perhaps overly assertive in that his interactions are almost always typified by tenacious, candid, and confrontational overtones. His over-assertive style is obscuring how others see many of his grounded traits. Ken could attend to others with active listening in order to demonstrate empathy. He could be mindful of his nonverbal demeanor, conveying a respectful, affable tone. He could also draw on his strategic ability—his thoughtfulness, intuition, insight, and anticipatory sense—to be more responsive. By accessing these engaging traits, Ken will begin to experience better grounded strength.

Grounded Leadership, Ownership, and Accountability

One of the most common complaints I hear from leaders is that there is a lack of ownership and accountability in their people, especially the farther down in the organization they go. Ken faces this problem at his organization. He is trying to change the culture to one of ownership and accountability. Making favorable initial impressions by demonstrating composure, approachability, and genuineness are invaluable postures to promote ownership and accountability in people. Taking the time to focus again and again on initial impressions through behavior rehearsal will help Ken secure the mindset that he needs within his organization. Through accessing engaging traits, Ken will not only convey better initial impressions, but his reputation will begin to improve as well. Greater depth in both of these areas of grounded leadership will lay the foundation for Ken to drive better ownership and accountability. With such a foundation he can then also look across the model to the alter-brain behavior **transformational** in putting desired changes in motion.

Ken's GROUNDED Style Shift Summary

High scores: *Pragmatic, cautious, questioning, established*

Alter-brain depth targets: *Composed, approachable, genuine, stable, loyal, trustworthy*

Tools: Deep breathing, behavior rehearsal, active listening

Alter-brain breadth target: To modify overly-assertive posture with a style shift to **engaging** (traits *listening, respectful, empathic*) and a leverage of **strategic** strengths (traits *intuitive, thoughtful, insightful, anticipatory*) in making the **engaging** shift

---

Like Ken, many leaders have difficulty with assertiveness. With the performance pressures of today, it is easy to understand how assertiveness can be over-attended-to for some. **Assertive**, the fourth and final MEGA Mind behavior, when exercised properly, can and will take a leader to successful execution.

ASSERTIVE

> Nothing in the world can take the place of persistence. Persistence and determination alone are omnipotent. The slogan 'Press On' has solved and always will solve the problems of the human race.
>
> —*Calvin Coolidge*

Across the globe, Vice Premier Wu Yi works to lead her country through unprecedented growth in the face of mammoth challenges. One of four vice premiers for the People's Republic of China, Wu Yi's role is seated in the economy. With a long and distinguished leadership record, Wu Yi's positions have included deputy mayor of Beijing, deputy minister of foreign economic relations and trade, minister of international trade and economic cooperation, and now vice premier. Her winning combination is said to be her unyielding character and definitive stance, hallmarks of an assertive leader. To be an assertive leader is to be upfront, direct, and determined in order to get the desired results. The traits of **ASSERTIVE** leadership are:

Purposeful – being determined and definite in your goals

Confident – being assured about your capability to reach desired goals

Tenacious – being unrelenting

Driven – staying determined to reach goals and get results

Delegating – able to assign and resource the work appropriately

Decisive – able to make sound decisions

Courageous – being willing to face challenges and difficulties

Candid – being upfront and direct

Confrontational – able to work through conflict

Closure-seeking – seeing things through and pushing for conclusions

Looking at Wu Yi relative to those traits we see an exemplar. She was recognized by *Time* magazine as one of the 100 Most Influential People of 2004 for her courageous and decisive leadership during the SARS crisis. *Time* referred to her as the "goddess of transparency" for her candid confrontation of the crisis. More recently, she was named second among *Forbes* magazine's Most Powerful Women in the World. *Forbes* notes both her purposeful involvement internationally and closure-seeking stance in continuing to assist China through its internal issues and opportunities. At home, Wu Yi's drive, confidence, and tenacity netted her the media nickname "iron lady of China." We can only assume that in accomplishing what she has, Wu Yi is also a sound delegator, able to assign tasks and involve others in the most effective way. As fierce as Wu Yi has been described, we see little if any evidence in her descriptions of being ill-mannered or aggressive per se. She is seen as tough, capable, and unstoppable in the appropriate senses of those words.[5]

Assertive leadership is often contorted, especially in today's business climate. There is an increasing pattern of micromanaging and harshness, the morphed version of assertiveness that should not be mistaken for true assertive leading. True assertive leadership is about being in charge in order to reach goals and attain success, and doing so in a way that is professional and morally sound. It is not about running over the top of others, being rude or aggressive, or putting your needs ahead of others. Such behaviors generate negative gains for you and those around you. Over time, others become desensitized to your impact. They may comply, but it will be with the mindset "because I have to." Their "have to" mindset requires constant negative energy on your part to maintain. The impact on you personally is disenfranchising. In essence, your true leadership privilege is usurped.

David Dotlich and Peter Cairo, in their book *Why CEOs Fail*, examine behavioral elements to leadership success. Based on the work of Robert Hogan, eleven leadership derailers are examined through a case study approach. Several of the identified derailers contribute to ineffective assertiveness. Arrogance, for example, is one derailer. Arrogance is the belief that you invariably know more than the rest of us. When the assertive leader acts from a posture of arrogance, the leader's assertive impact is thwarted. Volatility is a second derailer. Volatility is described as being prone to emotional outbursts and mood swings.[6] Your gut check for assertiveness-run-amok is whether or not your behavior devalues others. It is important for outspoken, take-charge leaders to know and see the difference between being assertive and taking one's assertiveness too far.

Effective Assertiveness: The Real Deal

Getting the job done but getting it done well while respecting those around you is what effective assertiveness is all about. To illustrate effective assertiveness, meet Dr. Ron, who is owner and founder of a large, suburban medical practice. Dr. Ron is a strong, forceful surgeon who settles for nothing less than perfection, and those around him love working with him. So what does Dr. Ron have that makes him able to push others to the limit in a way that they can accept?

Assertive leadership starts with a sense of purpose. Dr. Ron is masterful at launching the day. Perhaps it is his love for the game of golf, but whatever it is, he tees up each and every task with the same precision he uses to tee up his golf ball. Put another way, he introduces responsibilities, as well as the day at hand, definitively. In addition to being purposeful, Dr. Ron is adept at four additional assertive traits: he is confident and tenacious. He is driven and delegating. Used in this sense, assertive confidence means that you portray competence in the moment. It also means that you have a desire to always be better. To be tenacious is to stick firmly to a plan and be able to execute on that plan through motivating force. The assertive leader is also able to delegate tasks and effectively leverage resources. The behaviors in the first half of the assertive trait spectrum—purposeful, confident, tenacious, driven, and delegating—are the *foundational* assertive traits. They enable a leader to set initiatives in motion and keep then moving forward.

We can see that Dr. Ron and his team perform with excellence. He continually pushes for next-level performance. He expresses passion for the work and getting it right rather than arrogance about his ability. He drives to a fierce schedule with precision and excellence. Everyone on the team has a valued role to play. At the end of the day, team members feel they have worked hard and accomplished something. They feel pushed to be better, not beaten down or dejected. This is how you achieve foundational assertive excellence.

The next five assertive traits—decisive, courageous, candid, confrontational, and closure-seeking—represent how well a leader deals with issues and setbacks along the way. As such, these traits fall under the heading *reactive* assertiveness. Dr. Ron would receive high marks for both decisiveness and courage. He is more than able to make decisions and face difficulties. He is candid, open, direct, and honest. Those around him know clearly where they stand. He is appropriately confrontational and seldom loses his cool. He confronts by talking through an issue. He is a closer, following through and leaving nothing undone.

Dr. Ron is highly assertive, but not to the point of being overplayed or derailed. The reason for this is his right brain balance. As strong as he is in assertive ability, he is equally strong at engaging. He is exceedingly empowering, motivational, and charismatic. Dr. Ron is able to push others to the degree that he does because of his ability to shift style and engage them as well.

Peter's Assertive Style

Our case study Peter would be seen as possessing favorable assertive skills. That impression, however, would come from his team and would be less shared by his peers. Peter's team sees him as a solid, direct, and respectful force. As discussed in Chapter 3, Peter has difficulty relating to his peer group. Peter's assertive leadership will, therefore, be assessed here from the vantage point of his peer group in order to assist him with this situational difficulty.

With respect to foundational assertive leadership and his peers, Peter is seen favorably for the most part. They would say that he is *purposeful*.

Peter is certainly experienced as being determined to do what he sets out to accomplish. He is *confident*, portraying a capability about the work. He is both unrelenting and determined. Once he begins something he stays with it to the end and as such is both *tenacious* and *driven*. Peter scored low in his peers' eyes for the trait *delegating*, able to resource the work, in that they see him as unable to look to those outside of his immediate team as work sources.

With respect to reactive assertiveness and his peers, Peter struggles with three assertive traits: *decisive, confrontational*, and *candid*. For each of these aspects of reactive assertiveness, Peter's peer group would give him a low rating because he does not share information or include them in the decision-making process, and he avoids them altogether when conflict occurs. They would rate him as moderate in the other two aspects of reactive leadership, *courageous* and *closure-seeking*. Exclusive of conflict, he tackles most other difficulties head on, and exclusive of closure with respect to interpersonal matters, he sees to it that other more task-related matters are dealt with.

Specific areas of peer-assertive difficulty for Peter, most interpersonally based, are that his decisions do not take into account his peer group's circumstances or opinions; he avoids confrontations and issue resolution with them, instead working around them; and he lacks candor, leaving his peer group too often in the dark. Peter's assertive ratings relative to working with peers are shown in Figure 4.4.

Peter's four assertive difficulties with his peer group are interpersonally based. He fails to interact with his peers regarding delegation opportunities outside of his team, and as the work progresses and problems arise, Peter disengages from them all the more. Since this problem is situational, existing within Peter's peer group and not with others, he needs to understand the root cause. In Chapter 3, we saw that Peter had difficulties with inquisitiveness and empathy and that he lacked specific depth in multicultural awareness. Peter appears to be backing away from his peers because of his and their differences in style and approach. When problems arise he is uncomfortable with them, so he disengages.

Parallel Paths

Peter's remediation could take two parallel paths. While working on developing overall inquisitiveness, empathy, and cultural awareness to develop the behavior **engaging** as outlined in Chapter 3, Peter could put a structured chaining plan into effect, taking small progressive steps to begin to develop more comfort with his peers, his assertive weakness. Peter can begin with the team member he feels most comfortable with and carve out regular time to speak or meet with that individual monthly.

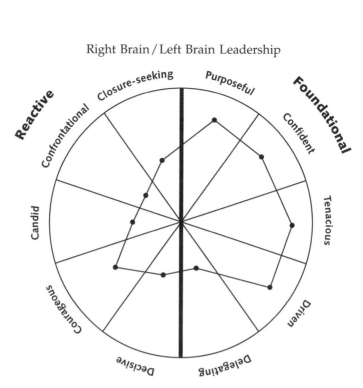

Figure 4.4 Peter's Ratings for Traits of ASSERTIVE Leadership With His Peer Group

Each month he would add encounters with the next most comfortable person. A structured plan will ground Peter in his preference for order.

Since his assertive difficulties are, in part, communication-based, to support his efforts further Peter should shift style and draw from the expressive trait *prepared* and the methodical trait *focused* for help. Peter should construct a brief outline for conversations with each peer. The conversations would have three parts: 1) briefing them on status updates and other relevant matters; 2) asking them for updates and perspectives; 3) identifying and discussing decisions that need to be made. By adding the elements of preparedness and focus to his conversations, Peter would make his contacts with his peers less ambiguous and more certain. He engages his left brain methodical ability to focus, along with his left brain expressive skill in preparation, and applies both to a right brain engaging circumstance. Using small progressive steps adds an additional element of structure and will make it easier for Peter to be successful. Disciplining himself to have contact with his peers over and over again provides the behavior rehearsal necessary for his interactions with them to become non-events. Grounded in a preferred left brain style, he works in a parallel manner to support his right brain development. As he does so, he develops greater depth in the left brain behavior **assertive**. Peter's alter-brain behaviors are in full swing.

Peter's ASSERTIVE Style Shift Summary

High scores: *Purposeful, confident, tenacious, driven*

Alter-brain depth targets: *Delegating, decisive, confrontational, candid* (Note: as Peter addresses his depth trait targets—delegating, decisive, confrontational, and candid—his moderate scores on *courage* and *closure-seeking* should also improve)

Tools: Chaining, behavior rehearsal

Alter-brain breadth target: To shift style to **expressive** (trait *prepared*) and **methodical** (trait *focused*) to support chaining activity. Concurrent development work to become more **engaging** (traits *inquisitive, empathic*) will also support his assertive interactions with peer group

---

The Under-Assertive

Not all of the problems with assertiveness come from overplayed strengths. Some leaders like Angela need to work to bolster their assertive skills. In Chapter 3, we learned how Angela's difficulty confronting others undermined her effectiveness. If you believe that you are under-assertive, there are several points to keep in mind. Today's work climate is typified by a heightened sense of urgency. Lower levels of assertiveness in a leader can give the impression that the leader does not share that urgency. The work climate is also characteristically tougher than in the past. Lesser assertiveness can give the impression that you are not able to make tough calls, that you do not push your teams hard enough, that you are incompetent, that you are evasive, or that you will not be able to get the job done. While these impressions may or may not be accurate, when the results are not there, *you* will look like the reason.

Leaders who score low on one or more assertive traits should look carefully at their situation and be clear about the perceptions others have of them. You may be able to go along for some time without an issue, but when the business falls on hard times, you will be more vulnerable. All things considered, underdeveloped assertive abilities need to be a development priority. To help with becoming more assertive, the left brain approach would be to use the behavior rehearsal tool. Some use role playing as a means for this kind of practice and enlist the help of others to act out the situation in order to practice the desired response. This is helpful as you can then get feedback from those assisting you along the way.

Just as Peter used small progressive steps and behavior rehearsal (left brain approaches) to help him become more engaged with uncomfortable colleagues, you can use small progressive steps and behavior rehearsal to increase your assertiveness. Start with situations that are not at all threatening and practice assertive responses with those. Then, slowly move up to more and more difficult encounters or circumstances. The point is to get yourself used to making assertive statements, taking a stand, and not backing down, by doing it slowly and then practicing it over and over again.

A right brain tool for becoming more assertive is to repeat the activity Madison did in Chapter 3 to better understand her risk-taking, the reflection. The intent would be to try to be more assertive in a less difficult situation in order to better understand the nature of your under-assertiveness and from there gain insight that could lead you to your next steps.

There are many assertiveness training programs available to help you as well. They are offered through company human resource departments and a variety of self-help books. Coaches and mentors can also help support you with this or other development initiatives.

A Checklist for Left Brain Inspiration

To close this chapter on left brain leadership, we go back to the beginning of the chapter to a left brain tool, the checklist. The checklist will serve as your left brain inspiration, providing points for consideration and motivation. Using checklists for cursory evaluation can encourage you. In this case, the checklist is being used to encourage your left brain leadership development. Go down the checklist of left brain leadership traits in Figure 4.5 and place a plus (+) next to those you excel at, an equal sign (=) next to those traits you have some skill in, and a minus (-) next to those traits you are less adept at. This left brain checklist will guide you in development of behaviors that are methodical, expressive, grounded, and assertive—your MEGA Mind.

Your MEGA Mind Checklist

Methodical
❏ Task oriented
❏ Detail oriented
❏ Organized
❏ Effective
❏ Focused
❏ Procedural
❏ Sequential
❏ Logical
❏ Analytical
❏ Factual

Expressive
❏ Prepared
❏ Articulate
❏ Coherent
❏ Concise
❏ Erudite
❏ Presentable
❏ Passionate
❏ Personable
❏ Persuasive
❏ Interesting

Grounded
❏ Composed
❏ Approachable
❏ Genuine
❏ Pragmatic
❏ Cautious
❏ Questioning
❏ Stable
❏ Loyal
❏ Established
❏ Trustworthy

Assertive
❏ Purposeful
❏ Confident
❏ Tenacious
❏ Driven
❏ Delegating
❏ Decisive
❏ Courageous
❏ Candid
❏ Confrontational
❏ Closure-seeking

Figure 4.5 Left Brain Leadership Behaviors and Traits

Unless the book is the sole personal property of the reader, this checklist should be photo-copied before use, and the original copy as bound in the book should not be altered in any way. Electronic copies can be accessed at www.leadlifeinstitute.com.

CHAPTER 5

THE PLUS FACTORS: RESILIENT

When you meet someone better than yourself, turn your thoughts to becoming his equal. When you meet someone not as good as you are, look within and examine your own self.

—*Confucius*

Right brain and left brain behaviors enable you to look after the work and to look after others, but who is looking after you? The Plus Factors, **resilient** and **savvy**, have the view of *looking in* and focusing on what you need to know in order to look after yourself. These two guiding behaviors are right- and left-brain enhancing and have direct bearing on how well you execute the other eight behaviors. Because of their pivotal role in right and left brain behavior effectiveness, the Plus Factors are key players in your leadership success.

The Plus Factor **resilient** addresses how well you are able to deal with difficult times and stretch yourself beyond existing capabilities. Being resilient is critical to your sense of accomplishment and well-being. When you are at your best, physically and mentally, you are more likely to feel satisfied. The Plus Factor **savvy** reflects the political side of impact. **Savvy** enables you to understand the social networks operating around you and secure the support necessary to influence desired audiences with greater success. Plus Factors encourage you to take stock in how well you are truly managing yourself. When leveraged properly, Plus Factors can help you endure in even the most tumultuous of times. The Plus Factors are described as follows:

Resilient: to possess the optimal physical and mental functioning, stamina, and mindset

Savvy: to sense and respond appropriately to the organization's cultural climate; to get things done in a way that advances both you and those individuals and organizations you are affiliated with

A Matter of Balance

> A great secret of success is to go through life as a man who never gets used up.
>
> —*Albert Schweitzer*

How do we, in Schweitzer's terms, go through life and never get used up? It's all a matter of balance. A number of dualities have been presented thus far: the dual right and left brain, the duality in emotional response, the central nervous system's dual check and balance. Success in any and all aspects of life is often a matter of duality and, as such, a matter of balance. Success comes from a dynamic interplay between differing, yet complementary aspects of the whole. Being resilient is no different. To become more resilient you need to master a balance, a certain dynamic interplay that centers on your energy. Resilience comes from the successful balance between how you expend and replenish both physical energy and mental energy. Physical energy encompasses your health and fitness. Mental energy is more complex. It is about your thought processes, how you come to conclusions, and how you ultimately react.

Who comes to mind when you think of being resilient? Some think of remarkable athletes who have pushed themselves to the limit—Lance Armstrong, for example, the famous cyclist known not only for his consummate athletic success, but more notably for his ability to win against his fiercest opponent, cancer. When thinking of the resilient, we may think of leaders and activists like Mahatma Gandhi, Nelson Mandela, and Martin Luther King Jr., whose lifelong crusades against injustice made them international symbols for freedom. We may think of women leaders from Queen Elizabeth I to Susan B. Anthony, Elizabeth Cady Stanton, Eleanor Roosevelt, Billie Jean King, and Hillary Clinton, who led and lead in the fight for gender equality. There are countless inspirations to cite, each with differing degrees of physical and mental strength. When pushed to the limit, the resilient endure, in part, by virtue of their ability to effectively manage their energy.

The Energy Model

In the model for right brain / left brain leadership we think of energy in terms of having three defining features:

- Initiation – how we activate and motivate ourselves
- Funneling – what we do and how we do it
- Recovery – our health, wellness, and rejuvenation

Each of the ten resilient traits supports one of these features. Figure 5.1 shows them in an energy model. The ten traits of **RESILIENT** leadership are:

Positive – having constructive focus on opportunities and possibilities

Emotionally sound – able to cope with stress and difficulties as demonstrated by your behavior

Clear thinking – able to sort through confusions, block out distractions, and think freely

Tolerant – being accepting of differences

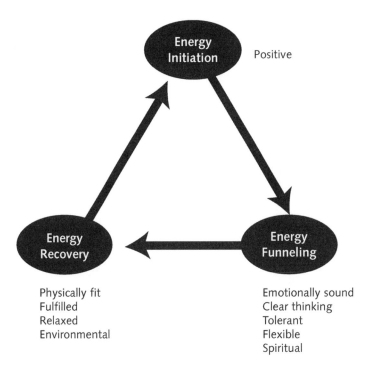

Initiation–how we activate and motivate ourselves
Funneling–what we do and how we do it
Recovery–our health, wellness and rejuvenation

Figure 5.1 Energy Model for Traits of RESILIENT Leadership

Flexible – being willing to adjust or accommodate when necessary

Spiritual – seeing beyond yourself to how you contribute in a broader sense; accountable to a greater good

Physically fit – practicing sound lifestyle habits; aware of and managing your health

Fulfilled – feeling a sense of accomplishment and satisfaction about your life

Relaxed – able to decompress from stress

Environmental – making nature a part of your personal and professional development

Energy Initiation

Energy initiation is supported by the trait *positive*, your constructive focus on opportunities and possibilities. To initiate your energy you need positive momentum. The resilient trait *positive* provides such momentum. Being positive in this sense has two components. The first is physical activation, which involves readying your body for the demands of the day. When you awake, get out of bed, and begin to move around, your blood circulation increases and physical activation begins. Physical activation can be enhanced by concerted movement of your extremities and by light stretching. It can be further aided by an action that works both sides of your brain, such as a hand-eye coordinated movement. Drinking water is a natural energy accelerant and will also facilitate physical activation.[1]

The second component to the trait *positive* is a favorable attitude, specifically, a mindset poised for success. In the book *Attitude 101: What Every Leader Needs to Know,* Ken Maxwell writes about the importance of attitude. Consider the following statements by Maxwell:

> For some, attitude presents a difficulty in every opportunity; for others it presents an opportunity in every difficulty.
>
> Your attitude and your potential go hand in hand.
>
> Attitude is always a player on your team.[2]

Maxwell describes attitude as the most important determinant of leadership success. In his first statement, we see two opposing attitudes: glass half empty or half full. In the second quote, we see a connection between attitude and potential, that given the right attitude almost anything is possible. In the third statement, we see that attitude is a resource. We need only employ it to reap its benefits.

Setting your attitude is a matter of locus of control. Are you in control of your life or is it in control of you? Surely there are things that happen that may be out of your control. However, rest assured that your attitude is something you are in complete control of. You could use a phrase or symbol to cue yourself to a favorable attitude. Think for a moment about the attitude that would have the greatest positive impact on your day or one that would help you cope with difficult times ahead. Jot down your thoughts. Now think about what it would take for you to act from that attitude. What would cue you? I keep a copy of Maxwell's book close by. It is a small, hardcover book with at-a-glance inspirations. The book itself has become my attitude cue. Remember that your attitude is your choice. You have the power to select it and put it into effect.

Energy Funneling

Energy funneling encompasses what we do and how we do it. It looks at our interactions and approaches. Energy funneling is facilitated by the resilient traits *emotionally sound, clear thinking, tolerant, flexible,* and *spiritual.* To be emotionally sound, you need to be aware of what triggers your emotions, both positive and negative, and ensure that your reactions are appropriate. Clear thinking means that you are attuned to and understand information that is available to you and that you draw sound conclusions. Being tolerant and flexible allows you to function from a greater range, accepting differing perspectives and being willing to accommodate or adapt when necessary. Spiritual in this sense speaks to a greater accountability and purpose, that as a leader you are here to contribute not only to your work, but to the greater good.

Energy Recovery

Energy recovery looks at your health, wellness, and rejuvenation. It looks at short-term rejuvenation—how you recover throughout the day or at the end of a long week. Energy recovery also looks at your over-all longevity. Four resilient traits comprise energy recovery. They are *physically fit* (your health and habits), *fulfilled* (how satisfied you are with your life), *relaxed* (how you decompress and unwind), and *environmental* (your involvement with nature). While *physically fit, fulfilled,* and *relaxed* are easily understood, *environmental* requires further elaboration.

Environmental is about our connection to and participation in the natural world. Nature is an aspect of resilient leadership for several reasons. Communing with nature, being outdoors, and breathing fresh air, immersed in natural beauty, feels great. It is relaxing. Far from man-made constructs and from the intellectual demands of work, we experience a sense of peace and well-being. Connecting with a natural environment stimulates our senses as we encounter new colors, sights, smells, sounds, and touches. Nature's grandeur helps us better see our place in the world, informing our perspective. The serene setting lends to introspection and reflection. As our natural world gives to us in this manner, we should then be more likely to care for it in return.

Case Review: Resilient Dichotomies

Angela's Resilient Challenges

Now that you have seen the ten traits of the guiding behavior **resilient** in the context of the energy model, let's look at two of our leadership cases, Ken and Angela, who have very different resilient strengths and development needs. Angela's resilient ratings grouped by energy initiation, funneling, and recovery are shown in Figure 5.2.

Figure 5.2 shows that Angela is strong in terms of her energy initiation and in most areas of energy funneling. Angela's greatest development opportunities are in the area of energy recovery. Her scores show that she is higher in areas involving interaction with others. She is *positive*. She begins the day in good form with an attitude poised for success and good physical momentum. She is known for being *emotionally sound*, not at all prone to moodiness or volatility. She approaches everyone with

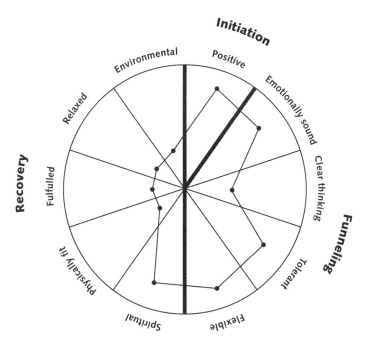

Figure 5.2 Angela's Ratings for Traits of RESILIENT Leadership Grouped by Energy Role

a *tolerant* and *flexible* mindset. She is accepting of differences and willing to make accommodations. She is highly *spiritual* through both her formal religious commitment and also her devotion to her neighborhood community.

On those traits that reflect how she cares for herself, she shows much lower ratings. Her *physically fit* score is low, as is her score on *fulfilled*. She has a number of chronic health issues to which she is not sufficiently tending. Her eating habits contribute in part to her health difficulties. She is committed to helping others, but at the end of the day her own happiness suffers. She has difficulty getting *relaxed* and, while she has several hobbies, she does not exercise or participate in any other stress-relieving measures. She is low on *environmental*, not yet realizing how nature can add to her life. Her lowest score is on *clear thinking*.

Self-Care Tools

The Questionnaire

Angela needs to initiate a process of self care, beginning with her health. A questionnaire developed for resilience work with our clients can be her first tool. It is called **HEALTH** Cues, and it assesses **H**abits, **E**nergy, **A**ctivities, **L**imitations, **T**hemes, and **H**eredity. The HEALTH Cues questionnaire assists clients in gaining an overall health perspective. This questionnaire should not be used as a substitute for professional medical care or advice but should be used as a way to begin to gather information about your current health and fitness. Answer for yourself the questionnaire below.

HEALTH Cues Questionnaire

Habits – Comment on your health habits, in particular, your sleep patterns, diet, and exercise. Note anything atypical; for example, do you smoke, work unusual hours, have exposure to any chronic stressors? Points to consider regarding your habits:

- Sleep – If you are not sleeping well, this is something to address. Sleep is your body's first line of defense in helping the brain and heart function normally. Consult your doctor to discuss sleep disturbances, insomnia being the most common, as insomnia can stem from a number of factors like anger, anxiety, depression, pain, illness, and even positive anticipation. Resist treating the problem symptomatically without proper medical evaluation and guidance.[3]

- Diet – When examining diets, look for an abundance of fresh foods that are easily digested, balanced, and high in nutrients and water content, as well as low in processed sugars and non-healthy fats. Evaluating diets is highly subjective and needs to take into account each individual's goals, desires, lifestyle, and medical issues. Again, consulting your medical professional is the starting point for questions you have or changes you seek with respect to diet, especially if weight loss is intended.

- Exercise – Exercise plans are also subjective and driven by individual needs and health conditions. Many options exist to give desirable health benefits, whatever your preferences or needs are. Be that as it may, some form of exercise is needed for all of us, not only for our health, but for promoting and maintaining energy. One can be fairly creative with an exercise plan once the available options are known. Consulting your doctor and a recommended fitness specialist to devise the best possible plan for you is advisable. Health, wellness, and medical SMEs are critical to your physical fitness planning. There is a glut of information out there about health, fitness, and wellness, much of which is unsubstantiated and none of which takes into consideration your personal health circumstance. The prudent thing to do is have a physician and other health and wellness specialists involved who can advise you properly.

Energy – Comment on your energy levels throughout the day. To begin to identify your energy management needs, look for patterns or trends. Your goal is to keep your energy on a relatively even keel with appropriate ups and downs. What you are looking to remedy are pronounced crashes, especially at times when you need to be more vital.

Activities – What do you do for enjoyment, growth, and enhancement; what are your hobbies; how do you vacation; what makes you laugh; what gives you pleasure; how do you continue to learn and take in knowledge, expanding your abilities in and out of work?

Limitations – What are you unable to do from a health perspective and why?

Themes – Do you notice any patterns to your health, that is, proneness to recurring health problems, or greater likelihood of health issues at certain times of the year or under certain circumstances?

Heredity – List family health concerns or strong suits.

Just Relax

Completing this questionnaire will assist Angela in better understanding her health circumstance and in identifying potential health, fitness, and wellness targets. Angela is currently under a great deal of stress. She has always had difficulty relaxing, and the recent pressures at work have made matters worse. Relaxation is a matter of calming the mind and body. A calm mind comes from refocusing your thoughts. Sensory aids can help. Sensory aids are pleasant sights, sounds, smells, tastes, and tactile sensations that quiet the mind. We all want a room with a view. Music is said to calm the savage beast, so too the haggard executive. We use lavender in lotions to help us sleep. We label certain menu items as comfort foods. These are all indications of sensory aids at work. Interesting to note is that the more sensory aids you employ together, the greater the relaxation experience. Called multi-sensory experiences, when you light a candle, put on soft music, and sit down to a sumptuous dinner, you are on your way to a more relaxed mind.

Our mind also relaxes through the practice of meditation. Meditation is accomplished through quiet concentration. When you meditate you focus solely on your thoughts, providing a momentary disconnect from the world around you. The benefit of meditation as a relaxation activity is that it also serves to focus the mind better, not just relax it. As such it can promote clarity, insight, and intuition. Meditation has even been described as creativity enhancing.[4]

Relaxing our body is to a large extent about relieving muscle tension. When we experience stress, our muscles tense. There are many activities that can relieve muscle tension. Therapeutic massage manipulates your muscles to help them heal from an over-taxed state. Energy recovery activities also help both your mind and body relax. Angela could employ a number of simple energy recovery activities to assist her in feeling more relaxed. This sampling of activities can be done at home or at the office.

Energy Recovery Activities

- Use dynamic sitting. When seated for extended periods in meetings, at a desk, on planes, cars, and trains, our muscles experience added strain and fatigue. Dynamic sitting helps. This simply means moving your position. Get up and walk around or change position.

- Drink plenty of water. Water accelerates energy.

- Practice light stretching. Provided you have no physical injuries that the stretching would interfere with, light stretching is a great recovery activity. Working on the computer or talking for extended periods on the phone makes stretching all the more necessary to get your whole body circulation going and release tension in over-used areas. Consult a book or fitness specialist for stretching guidelines. For energy recovery benefits, stretching should be gentle. It is only intended to promote blood circulation and provide movement that will relieve fatigued muscles, not as a workout.[5]

- Practice deep breathing. It will help give you energy and relax you.

- Laugh. It is the best medicine for stress and a great form of relaxation.

- Practice guided power naps. This is a technique that takes less than fifteen minutes but can be extended slightly longer if you have the time. Sit comfortably in a quiet place where you won't be interrupted, close your eyes, begin deep breathing, and clear your mind of outside

thoughts. Sometimes it is helpful to put on soft music or to focus on a relaxing thought. As you feel yourself settling into a calmer state you can begin to relax your body one segment at a time. Relax your body from the waist down by breathing and focusing your mind on that body segment. You can say to yourself, "I am relaxing my lower body." Continue to breathe and move your attention to your midsection. Focus on your breathing and relax your midsection. Repeat this process for your neck, shoulders, and arms, then for your head. Take one final deep breath and as you do, relax your entire body into the chair. Slowly open your eyes. The guided power nap is as refreshing as an actual midday nap. You should feel relaxed, but alert, when you are through.[6]

Meditation and Clarity

The aspect of energy funneling where Angela scored lowest was clear thinking. Angela simply needs to have time alone to think. She is known as someone who is at all times accessible, leaving little or no time at work or at home to process her thoughts. Clear thinking is best accomplished in solitude. The practice of meditation described earlier as a way to help Angela relax is the perfect solitary tool to both relax her and improve thought clarity. Meditating in a natural setting would address her additional low score on *environmental*, giving her the added benefits nature affords. Found to promote good health, meditation could further serve as a fitness practice for her. Learning to meditate is probably best accomplished through SMEs (with personal instruction or using books or tapes to support your learning).

On Fulfillment and Values

Lastly, Angela scored low on the trait *fulfilled*. As Angela attends to her health, relaxation, and thought clarity, her fulfillment should improve as well. Fulfillment issues can be greatly affected by problems in these other areas. Additionally, fulfillment can be impacted by a number of other factors. Some say that fulfillment and attitude go hand and hand, that a positive attitude increases one's fulfillment. Others believe that fulfillment is tied directly into our values, that if we are living in conflict with our values our fulfillment will suffer. This is referred to as a form of incongruence. If we are working in an environment or culture at odds with our values or are involved with individuals whose beliefs are discrepant from our own, we experience a disparity that compromises our ability to feel truly satisfied.

That is not to say we should only surround ourselves with people who have everything in common with us. Diversity in interactions and experiences is enhancing and resilience-building. However, if our fundamental values are at odds with our situation we can feel compromised, hence, unfulfilled. Values clarification assessments can help us identify what is important to us and help us sort through the favorable versus compromising circumstances in our lives. There are formal values assessments you could take to better understand this. You could also start exploring your values with the following tool.

Values Clarification Exercise

1. Initial drawing – Using colored markers or crayons, draw something that conveys what you value most on a blank sheet of paper. After you've completed the drawing, write a short paragraph to summarize what the drawing reflects.

2. Prompting questions – Next, answer the following questions.

   - Which three individuals do you admire most and why?
   - What three things are most important to you in life and why?
   - Brainstorm ten words or symbols that reflect how you think people should conduct themselves.
   - What three aspects of your life are most satisfying to you at the moment and why?
   - What three aspects of your life are least satisfying and why?
   - If you could do three things you've never done what would they be?
   - If you could be three things you have never been what would they be?

3. Synthesis – Look back over what you've drawn and written to identify themes. Write five to ten statements, in order of priority, that capture your themes. Statements should begin with the words, "I value...".

4. Reflection – Look over your value statements and see where there is congruence and incongruence between what you have written and your current life.

5. Actions – List three to five actions, things you can START, STOP, or CONTINUE doing to align your actions better with your values.

Angela has many options for becoming more resilient, and as she does her overall development as a leader will be assisted as well. Becoming more resilient will support her ability to deal with conflict and confrontation. When she is more physically fit, clear thinking, and relaxed, she will be enabled to address difficult situations from a greater position of strength. Her clear thinking also will assist her expressive capability, in particular, being more prepared and compelling. Through greater resilience, Angela can restore the enthusiastic sense that is her natural hallmark. Following is a summary showing Angela's depth style shift.

Angela's RESILIENT Style Shift Summary
High scores: *Positive, emotionally sound, tolerant, flexible, spiritual*
Alter-brain depth targets: *Physically fit, fulfilled, relaxed, environmental, clear thinking*
Tools: HEALTH Cues questionnaire, health, wellness and fitness SMEs, sensory aids, recovery activities, meditation, values clarification

Ken's Resilient Challenges

Moving from Angela to Ken, we see his ratings for resilient leadership in Figure 5.3. Ken and Angela are polar opposites. While Angela is lower in self care, Ken is lower in **resilient** areas that are more interactive.

Ken is high in *clear thinking, spiritual, physically fit, fulfilled,* and *environmental.* Ken's clear thinking is reflected in how he organizes his thoughts. He rarely speaks about something unless he has thought it through completely. He is also well able to resist distractions. Ken, like Angela, has a deep spiritual sense. He is active in his church and in giving

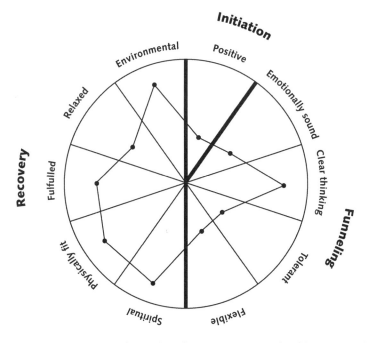

Figure 5.3 Ken's Ratings for Traits of RESILIENT Leadership Grouped by Energy Initiation, Funneling, and Recovery

back to his community. Both he and Angela feel a responsibility to help others on many levels. Ken is in excellent condition. He is physically fit and satisfied with his life, feeling fulfilled. His environmental spirit is seen in how much of his free time he spends outdoors. He and his family travel almost exclusively to natural vacation spots such as national parks. Ken finds these excursions instrumental in being able to return to work reinvigorated.

Ken is moderate on the trait *relaxed*. He knows how to decompress after stress but does not handle stress well in the moment. Short-term recovery is his issue. For assistance, Ken can practice the same recovery activities as Angela. Ken is low in areas of energy initiation and funneling, specifically the traits of *positive, emotionally sound, tolerant*, and *flexible*. Ken's difficulties with these traits are interrelated and need to be considered in consort.

Ken's problems begin with how he frames his day. His attitude is not properly set; it centers on wanting to be the best. His is an attitude of individual excellence. While one could argue that such an attitude is a positive, in Ken's case it reinforces a number of his behavioral negatives. It contributes to many of Ken's grounded leadership difficulties—to his lack of composure and approachability, to name two. His individualistic attitude is also contrary to one of the initiatives he was hired to correct. He is expected to build greater collaboration among his people. Ken needs to be a collaborative role model if he is to succeed at this directive.

Ken could begin his day in a different way. Presently, he wakes up, gets his coffee, and goes to the gym to exercise before heading to work. During his workout he begins to plan his day, focusing on what he wants and needs to accomplish. His self-absorbed attitude is reinforced by this morning regime. A different way for Ken to begin his day would be with an activity intended to move his mindset from "me" to "we."

Attitude Setting

To get Ken ready to move his mindset, he needs to allow himself fifteen extra minutes as he wakes up in the morning for an energy initiation activity called attitude setting. As Ken awakes he will pay attention to his breathing. Before getting out of bed, he will take several slow, deep breaths. Breathing in this manner will calm and slow him, giving his mind a chance to accept a new perspective on the day.

Whereas before Ken would wake up and jump out of bed with a hard-charging solitary focus, now he will initiate his energy with a collective mindset. When Ken awakes, he will sit quietly for a moment, focus on his breathing, and begin to think about the day ahead. He will consider the type of attitude that will help him convey positive thoughts to his team and the type of attitude that will enhance his own sense of teamwork.

Ken will think of the opportunities he has to engage others and of ways to make them a part of his planning. He can think of those who tend to cause him the greatest difficulty and of the attitude necessary to better work with them. Ken will take one final slow deep breath and resume his usual routine, calling to mind an attitude of the collective, working along with others.

Attitude setting is not just about being positive but about having the right attitude for the circumstance. It is about your expectations being better aligned with what you need to accomplish. If Ken's attitude is based on an expectation that he alone is driving the day, he starts off at a deficit. Ken doesn't work alone and cannot accomplish what he needs to without the collaboration of those around him. His expectation is unrealistic. More to the point, his expectation directly compromises five of the **resilient** traits. It compromises his ability to be positive, emotionally sound, tolerant, flexible, and relaxed in the moment. To be more on target, Ken's attitude needs to reflect others as an integral part of his success.

A Resilient Reframe

What about Ken's low scores on *tolerance*, *emotionally sound*, and *flexible?* There is a common denominator at work undermining Ken in these areas: self-criticism. Self-criticism is about how hard we are on ourselves. There is a direct correlation between how critical we are of ourselves and how critical we are of others. The more critical we are of others, the less tolerant we are. A critical nature can make us more rigid, thus less flexible. Being critical can increase our stress level, causing us to not cope well in the moment and be prone to emotional outbursts. This is Ken in a nutshell.

Ken drives himself hard. He is highly self-critical and this carries over to his interactions with others. A true perfectionist, his views are often clouded by over-attention to the details. When the slightest mistakes are made, he is unable to see the bigger and brighter potential. How can Ken orient his drive and desire for excellence in such a way that it works for him and not against him? How can he become more resilient in this regard? Ken can use a reframe. Just as Angela reframed resistance as a positive, he can reframe mistakes from an irritation to an opportunity.

Ken currently views mistakes as something to criticize, as setbacks, failures, or shortcomings. Remember that reframing works on the principle of logic, on rational thought. Ken can ask himself if it is rational or logical to expect that mistakes will never be made. The answer is no. He can also ask himself if any value can come from a mistake. The answer is yes. Mistakes often tell us more about our progress than success does. They tell us where our vulnerabilities are and can therefore be invaluable if we pay attention to them. It is not suggested that Ken invite error, but that he rather show acceptance of error, see it as an expected part of the process of change and also of basic human nature.

As Ken works to temper his critical nature he will begin to feel more emotionally stable and will come across as more emotionally sound. We saw in Chapter 4 that Ken had difficulty in his grounded leadership in part because of lack of composure. As he becomes more tolerant, so too will he become more emotionally sound, flexible, and therefore more composed. These three interrelated **resilient** traits will enhance Ken's grounded composure.

Ken's RESILIENT Style Shift Summary

High scores: *Clear thinking, physically fit, fulfilled, environmental, spiritual*

Alter-brain depth targets: *Positive, emotionally sound, tolerant, flexible, relaxed*

Tools: Recovery activities, attitude setting, reframing

Resilient as Right- and Left-Brain Enhancing

Through examination of Ken's development needs in the traits *tolerant, emotionally sound,* and *flexible,* we also see opportunity for a style shift from left to right brain. Ken's left brain methodical and assertive abilities are strong. He can plan and execute well; however, he is not as strong in being grounded. His resilient trait development to become more tolerant, flexible, and emotionally sound will help enable a style shift to the alter-brain behavior **engaging** in that his interactions with others will be more favorable. As his resilience improves and he shifts style to be more engaging, he will come across to others as more at ease, more composed, and thus more grounded.

Examining Ken's resilient trait development with respect to his attitude will show in even greater detail how Plus Factors are right- and left-brain enhancing. The change in Ken's attitude from the individual to the collective will instigate multiple style shifts from left brain to right. Three left brain behaviors, **methodical, expressive,** and **assertive,** are driving Ken's current attitude. Ken's work style is typified by his methodical nature. He likes to have structured plans in place and follow them. Ken is also expressive. He talks a lot and has a more difficult time listening. Ken is also highly assertive. He is tenacious in attaining results. Three right brain behaviors, **engaging, strategic,** and **innovative,** will be encouraged as Ken makes the attitude shift called for here. He will be shifting style from his left brain preferences to again focus on being more engaging.

Positioning himself to work with others rather than to direct them is the cornerstone of engaging leadership. Earlier in the book, Ken's strategic abilities were discussed. There he was seen as needing to be more broad-minded. Through his focus on a new attitude, he will become more collaborative, and as he does so, he will have the benefit of others' perspectives. At the same time, those perspectives should broaden his strategic skill set. The reframing activity he is being asked to perform involves a style shift to the experimental, a trait of innovative leadership. Ken's new attitude is right-brain enhancing.

Angela on the other hand will be making a shift from right to left. Angela needs to shift style from engaging to both methodical and assertive leadership. With respect to **methodical**, she needs to become more focused, especially in establishing her priorities. She tends to let others' needs overshadow what she needs or thinks best. Her own health care and wellness is one example of an overlooked priority. The health questionnaire she is being asked to complete will improve her focus and help her set necessary priorities. As she completes this left brain tool, she will work through the maze of information about her health and be able to zero in on where she should focus her attention. Angela could also benefit from being more logical and critical. She tends to err on the emotional side of issues. She is overly responsive. As she practices meditation and her thought clarity improves, so too will her logic and critical thinking. Free of distraction and able to stand on her own, the more objective possibilities may become illuminated for her. Angela's style shift will be left-brain enhancing.

Through examining Angela and Ken's **resilient** development we can see just how enhancing the Plus Factors can be.

The Spiritual Sense of a Leader

The trait *spiritual* is a fitting one to end this section with. *Spiritual* is defined in this context as seeing beyond yourself to how you contribute in a broader sense and are accountable to a greater good. It is important for leaders to see their impact extending beyond their formal assignments to how they give devotion, service, and commitment to something outside of themselves. It is important for leaders to feel accountable to the greater good, in an earthly sense and beyond. Why is being spiritual as described in this context a trait of **resilient**? Because it extends your leadership perspective, thereby extending you beyond your existing capability. This concept, that you are not only accountable for your work results but also for how you as a leader can make both the work culture and your world beyond work a better place, continues to set a new leadership bar for us to aspire to. Ken and Angela derive their spirituality from their religions and from giving to a greater good in an earthly sense in their local communities. Spirituality inevitably links us to others; it bonds us with those who share our beliefs and motivates us to have care and concern for those outside that sphere.

The intent here is not to get into philosophical or value-loaded discussions about what it means to be spiritual, but rather to suggest that leaders who both extend their contributions beyond their immediate realm and who feel accountable in a broader sense position themselves for greater growth and impact. The intent is also to suggest that two additional avenues exist in addition to religion and charity to build your spiritual sense as it is defined here. These avenues are right in front of us each and every day. They are the interactions we have with our children and with our elders.

I was facilitating a session for a team recently and the team leader, a top executive in the organization, relayed a poignant story. He told us that on his way to the session he dropped his young daughter off at school. On the ride she asked what he was going to be doing at work that day, and he told her he was going to an all-day team-building meeting with his group. She asked him what that was and why grown-ups needed to learn to work together. "Don't they already know how to do that, Dad?" she innocently asked. He found himself in an interesting discussion, explaining to a six-year-old why adults needed help working better together. This discussion shows the *spiritual* trait in action, helping a child understand life, conflict, and relationships. He said the discussion was not only helpful for his child, but it also helped crystallize for him why his team was there and what he hoped they would get out of their time together. This spiritual connection enhanced his ability to engage his team, strategize about the team's future, and transform the culture of his organization. Sharing the story with his team engaged and interested the group, providing an inspiring session kick-off.

At the other end of the developmental spectrum are the elderly. The elderly are as facilitative to spiritual development as are our children. My parents are in their seventies. My husband's parents are eighty-five and ninety years old. We consider our time with them precious. Our moments together can be difficult, but they are always enlightening. We find endless dichotomies at work in every interaction with our parents. Dichotomies exist between our self-pride and paying them the respect they have earned, between having to teach them how to operate the remote on their new television and learning from their ever-present wisdom. Conversations with an elder about what you are doing and why, given their lens and perspective, stretch us. Holding a discussion with them to help them cope with senescence stretches us further still as we are forced to confront the inevitability of our own mortality.

Cultures that value the young and old are by their very nature more spiritual. Thinking of ways that we can help, support, and learn from our young and old alike keeps us accountable on the most meaningful level of all and will make us better people and better leaders.

The descriptors "young" and "old" can also be thought of in less literal terms to mean those new and long-standing to our teams. Orienting our new members and validating our long-standing ones relative to how they come into our organizations and evolve out with care and dignity will make us better people and better leaders as well.

Resilient: Parting Thoughts

Becoming more resilient requires a low-key approach; it's not something to attack head on. The reason for this is that unlike the right and left brain behaviors, the Plus Factors evoke greater resistance. In order to become more resilient the emphasis is on you. Other behaviors are perceived to have more direct bearing on the work and as such take precedence. You may tend to put off attention to yourself. Because of this, you need to find ways to infuse **resilient** development into your day-to-day with small, unassuming actions. Begin by assessing yourself relative to the ten traits of **resilient**, looking for your greatest opportunity. Go after that one opportunity, incorporate a change, and move on to the next target. For example, something as easy as drinking more water throughout the day is a great place to start. Once you have progressed through two or three such opportunities you will begin to notice the benefits and become hooked, wanting to take your progress further.

Clients experiencing success with new resilient skills become believers because the impacts are so personally felt. Toting your purified water bottle and finding opportunities for a deep cleansing breath, you too will soon become hooked. Coworkers, family, and friends will begin to notice something different about you. They won't be quite able to pinpoint the change, but they will welcome it. Your changes will be unobtrusive, yet powerful. By caring better for yourself, you will come across better and feel stronger and more capable. You can now take your newfound robust image a step farther to develop the second Plus Factor, **savvy**.

CHAPTER 6

THE PLUS FACTORS: SAVVY

The right to be heard does not automatically include the right to be taken seriously.

—Hubert Humphrey

Angela Merkel is taken very seriously. This savvy leader has been quoted as saying: "I tend not to jump to quick conclusions. I prefer to go over things carefully to see where the traps could be lurking." Voted *Forbes* magazine's 2006 and 2007 Most Powerful Woman, Germany's chancellor has been noted for influencing broad factions in a global arena. She has engaged diverse groups at the G-8 (Group of Eight) Summit and in serving her turn as head of the European Union.[1] Merkel's scope of responsibility requires that she function well within varied and complex, politically charged circumstances. For most of us, our interactions are far less intricate. However, negotiating political landscapes and influencing key stakeholders is daunting, nonetheless. Aristotle once said, "Man is by nature a political animal."[2] While the word "political" has negative connotations for many of us, in developing greater savvy, politics are a reality we need to attend to.

Power, Perception, and Awareness

Savvy is defined in the Right Brain / Left Brain Leadership Model as the ability to sense and respond appropriately to the organization's cultural climate, to get things done in a way that advances both you and those individuals and organizations you are affiliated with. As such it is our external focus, what we need to attend to concerning the world in which we move.

In this chapter, we will examine three key elements of **savvy**: power, perception, and awareness. Power will be explored in terms of what it is, who has it, and what to do with it. We will look at how perceptions impact our savvy and then at what we need to know and why, our awareness. Power, perception, and awareness will be explained both as they apply to you (your image and how you come across) and to the cultures you operate within (what is valued, important, and respected). These two views, of you and of culture, will provide a complete picture of **savvy's** complexities and help us see how to better act and behave. Our two younger leaders, Madison and Peter, bring to light **savvy's** complexities in the challenges they face.

Embracing Savvy

As with the behavior **resilient**, developing greater savvy is something we resist. Those who are less savvy relate savvy to politics and politics to dishonesty. They find attention to savvy as unnecessary or compromising to their integrity and underplay the role of power in their ultimate success or failure. Individuals who are more political see moving away from their position as a loss of power, of being at a disadvantage. How can you be convinced away from these two extremes to attend to your savvy skills and to do so in a balanced manner, one that acknowledges the use of appropriate influence?

Begin by reframing your thinking. For those who see savvy as underhanded, consider savvy as prudent protection of both you and those you are involved with. For those not wanting to lose ground, think of the ground that can be gained from working along with others, both outwardly and behind-the-scenes, instead of working around or over them. Also think about the role perceptions and awareness have in your success by considering these questions: how and when have misperceptions caused you difficulty? What could/should you do about that? How and when have accurate perceptions worked to your advantage? How has being more aware helped you? More importantly, have you ever been blindsided, caught off guard, unaware, and unprepared? What, if anything, would you like to be more aware of right here, right now, concerning your work or your life? These are some of the many questions that can be addressed as your savvy improves.

Two Perspectives

To encourage you to embrace savvy, two perspectives from leadership and organizational development experts will be reviewed. One provides a means of self-protection and high-integrity influence. The other helps us understand and leverage subtle yet powerful opportunities to make a difference.

Rick Brandon and Marty Seldman provide the first perspective. In their book *Survival of the Savvy: High-Integrity Political Tactics for Career and Company Success,* they detail how politics and integrity can coexist, all while you learn to assess and improve your image and the image of your organization. Brandon and Seldman define organizational politics as "informal, unofficial, and sometimes behind-the-scenes efforts to sell ideas, influence an organization, increase power, or achieve other targeted objectives."[3] Their book was written to help individuals in organizations understand company politics and develop necessary, balanced, and enhancing positioning.

They explain that some of us expect our contributions to stand on their own merit, that we assume we can make an impact simply by virtue of what we accomplish. For others, much of what is done is crafted, intended to accomplish a desired outcome. Brandon and Seldman characterize these positions as ranging from less or under-political at one end of the spectrum to more or overly political at the other end. The expectation that our contributions will stand on their own merit is based on faulty and often naïve assumptions. It negates the political tides operating within the cultures to which we belong. Likewise, using circumstances for our own benefit to get ahead and make ourselves look good can be exploitive, particularly when it is done at the expense of others. They stress the need for balance between these two political styles in order to have impact that advances both you and the cultures you operate within.[4]

Joseph Badaracco's book *Leading Quietly: An Unorthodox Guide to Doing the Right Thing,* portrays an important view of leadership while also showing another perspective on savvy. Badaracco sees the greatest opportunity for impact to be through well-executed behind-the-scenes actions, as he refers to them, through which leaders can unassumingly make a difference. Badaracco studied this low-profile, high-impact brand of leading and offers eight principles to follow in becoming an inconspicuous savvy force. His principles showcase the subtle, often overlooked yet powerful contributions that are made by this brand of leader working day in and day out to mold actions into results.[5]

Badaracco's leaders are all around us. They can be seen in the manager whose team goes from a horrific day to a better day, when with deadlines looming she takes the time to congratulate the group while remaining inwardly focused on what is needed to make tomorrow even better. There is the new vice president who at the height of the mess he inherited remains steady yet unyielding. Brandon and Seldman's perspective deals with the prevailing realities of cultural norms, values, and expectations and how the resulting politics are forever a part of what gets done and rewarded. Badaracco looks to mastering what can be accomplished with well executed subtlety.

Case Review: Savvy Challenges

With this background in mind and through a broader understanding of power, perception, and awareness, Madison and Peter will be examined relative to their savvy development. The ten traits of **SAVVY** leadership are:

Astute – being perceptive concerning people and circumstances

Subtle – able to work indirectly to influence people and situations

Diplomatic – using tact in your sensitive interactions

Promotive – effectively lobbying for your and others' issues and recognition

Timely – being aware of the right moment to make a point or deal with an issue

Culturally oriented – being grounded in the culture of your group or organization and acting from that knowledge in how you influence those within that culture

Networking – developing personal and professional relationships that are mutually beneficial

Assimilating – able to integrate into groups, teams, or cultures

Coalition-building – bringing together those who share your causes, views, or involvements

Visible – being regularly seen

Madison's Savvy

Figure 6.1 shows Madison's savvy ratings. Her high ratings begin with *astute*. Madison can size up a situation or person very quickly. She is *diplomatic* in that when she addresses a sensitive matter or concern she carefully chooses her words so as not to offend or escalate the situation. She has a tactful manner in which she expresses her views. She is *culturally oriented*. Madison's parents were grounded in their family's heritage. They saw to it that she came to know and appreciate their rich ethnic culture. They were also open-minded by nature. That combination has always made her fascinated with cultural tendencies and differences. She translates that learning well to organizational culture, having a sense for what is valued and how to act and relate to those around her. An extension of her cultural interest is her *networking* ability. She seeks out personal and professional relationships. She is *assimilating*, able to take her interest in cultures and involvement with others and use both to integrate well into groups and teams. It is easy to understand why she is also rated high on *visible*. She is highly social, circulating around to frequently and informally touch base with others.

Her low scores are in the traits *subtle*, *timely*, *promotive*, and *coalition-building*. These low scores are rather typical for a young leader. She is extremely well-intending, yet she overlooks the political undercurrents at

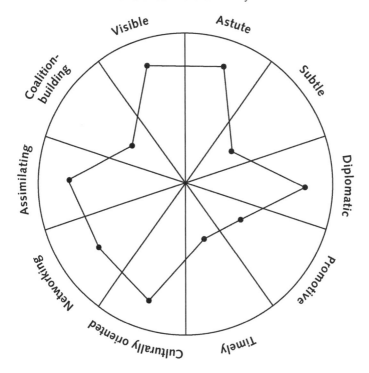

Figure 6.1 Madison's Ratings for Traits of SAVVY Leadership

work around her. She is passionate and enthusiastic, and while she considers what she says, she does not always think of the best timing for expressing her thoughts. She could benefit from sometimes introducing her points more indirectly. Being diplomatic, she may choose her words carefully, but she tends to deal with everything directly and in the moment. As such she is neither subtle nor timely. Though she is able to express her views, she is less apt to promote their acceptance. While she networks well, she does not take those relationships to the next level by forming specific coalitions.

Power as Influence

Madison has basic awareness and the potential for solid interpersonal engagement. She needs to apply those abilities in a way that gives her greater influence, greater power. Currently, she is influential because she is liked and respected. She needs to broaden her power to being recognized and followed as a stable leader. Power can be described as capacity to influence. It can vary in type and includes:

- Reward power – the ability to provide something that others value
- Coercive power – the ability to set limits or reprimand

- Legitimate power – authority by virtue of one's position
- Persuasive power – possessing and using information to convince
- Referent power – influence derived from being admired
- Expert power – possessing specific skills, knowledge, or expertise[6]

Greater power comes when you leverage each power type as a situation dictates, rather than limiting yourself to the forms of influence you are inclined to or comfortable with. Madison currently relies on referent and expert power in most situations. Understanding how to act from the other four power sources would enhance her influencing opportunities, hence her savvy. She would perhaps benefit from a power seminar or short course.

A Mentor for Madison

Madison has a sound foundation to build on as she develops her savvy leadership abilities. Understanding better about savvy from the authors mentioned in this chapter, as well as expanding her influencing skills, will move her along nicely. Madison would also benefit greatly from the wisdom of a mentor.

Mentoring programs take on many forms. All are intended to take high-potential individuals and support their next-level development by exposing them to the counsel of those more senior. It was mentioned that Madison has few leadership models to follow. A more experienced leader in her organization, one who is adept in organizational politics and understands Madison's specific savvy development needs, could assist her further. In particular, her mentor could help her better understand how to be more promotive and how she can perhaps use her existing networks to begin coalition-building.

Madison's style shift summary follows. On it you will see additional tools that will be amplified as the chapter unfolds.

Madison's SAVVY Style Shift Summary

High scores: *Astute, diplomatic, culturally oriented, networking, assimilating*

Alter-brain depth targets: *Subtle, timely, promotive, coalition-building*

Tools: Understand SMEs Brandon and Seldman and Badaracco's savvy perspectives, Himsel's feedback perspective, and Goleman's perspective on awareness, and attend a power seminar. Develop feedback skill with the help of a feedback log and journal, cuing, and deep breathing. Use chaining to assist with feedforward messages. Look to existing networks for coalition-building opportunities. Get a mentor.

Peter's Savvy

Peter, also a relatively young leader, is less interpersonally oriented than Madison. While he has good relationships with those he works for or those who work for him, he has few working relationships among his peers and needs to work on that. He also is in the process of developing better empathy skills and greater cultural awareness and understanding. Developing greater savvy is especially important to Peter as it will serve to complement and reinforce these and other development objectives.

Peter's ratings are seen in Figure 6.2. Peter is high on *astute, diplomatic,* and *timely*. He is perceptive, tactful, and aware of the right moment to raise issues. He is moderate on *visible* and *promotive*. He manages from the plant floor rather than from behind his desk and has regular contact with his boss. Peter is less visible across the organization, with his peers and colleagues. He is great at formal and informal recognition of those on his team who do well. As a plant manager, he knows the value of lobbying for issues and trying to get for his plant what it needs to perform well, though he tends not to go about it in the best way.

Peter's ratings on the five remaining savvy traits are low. He lacks *subtlety* and is often seen as blunt, too direct in trying to reach an outcome.

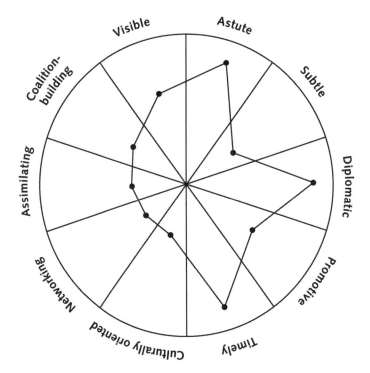

Figure 6.2 Peter's Ratings for Traits of SAVVY Leadership

He is not seen as *culturally oriented* or *assimilating*. He is perceived outside of his plant as aloof, working independent of others. Because of his autonomy he is not inclined toward *networking* or *coalition-building*. Peter is clearly someone on the under-political end of Brandon and Seldman's spectrum. He is focused on the work, on his immediate team, and on doing his best.

When viewed through the lens of the behavior **savvy**, the problems Peter has with his peer group take on a new dimension. Peter's lack of support from a critical organizational faction poses a direct threat to his success. Peter's present job requires collaboration outside of his team. Peter will be potentially vulnerable and hampered in his impact to the greater organization unless he develops his savvy. The level he has been promoted to and the manner in which he is expected to relate to his peers takes him out of a familiar framework. He can no longer operate independently, no matter how well he relates to his immediate boss and his team. He has to work cross-functionally. Peter is being thrust into the political arena whether he likes it or not. Peter needs to understand better how his interpersonal behaviors and interactions undermine his ability to succeed. Peter needs to better understand the role of perceptions.

Perception as Reality

Perceptions are potent determinants of others' opinions and images of you and your ability to influence, and they become reality for those forming them. As such they are critical to your savvy. Perceptions are interpretations of a person or situation. Several people involved in the same experience can have dramatically different interpretations. An easy way to illustrate this is to go to a movie with a group of people and at the end ask each of them what they thought of the film. Some will have loved it. Others will have hated it. Still others would have had a middle-of-the-road reaction. Ask around at work what ten individuals think of a certain coworker and see what responses you get. Ask the same individuals how they feel the company is doing this year. Again, you will get different responses.

While one aspect of perception is that it differs from individual to individual, another is that things are not always as they seem. Illusions are conscious attempts to alter our perceptions. Look at a brochure from a resort you are thinking of going to on vacation and compare it to what you find when you get there. Advertisements often enhance reality, deluding us into thinking we are getting more than we actually are. We create our own false perceptions as well. We see what we want to see. We hear what we want to hear. If we are to become better at savvy, at sensing and responding appropriately to cultural climates and getting things done in mutually enhancing ways—ways in which we look good and others benefit—we are going to have to get better at managing perceptions. To become better at managing perceptions we need to develop our awareness.

The Art of Awareness

For many years I taught a course in group dynamics. The course covered a range of topics including culture, assertiveness, active listening, verbal and nonverbal messages, relationships, power, conflict, perceptions, and awareness—a Savvy 101. In the section on awareness, three levels of awareness were noted: that which is readily apparent (what is out in the open), that which is not yet acknowledged (our blind spots), and that which is willfully concealed or hidden. The first concerns what most of us can observe and understand. Included in this category would be information or data that is factual in nature, such as how long George has worked in his present job or the company's total sales for last year. The second, our blind spots, is the single differentiator in savvy success and failure. We'll come back to that shortly. The final type of awareness, what is willfully concealed, can be either self-protective (a matter of information you consider private) or a hidden agenda.[7]

Awareness is the foundation of Gestalt psychology, a perspective based on the concept that the gestalt (the German word for "whole") is greater than the sum of its parts. Gestalt psychology emphasizes an accurate view of reality, personal responsibility, and the ability to govern outcomes. This perspective further emphasizes attention to the present, making the present what we want and need it to be. An adequate present is attained through understanding past experiences and implications, by bringing unpleasant recollections to closure, and by being realistic in our hopes for the future.[8] There are tie-ins from the Gestalt perspective to our leadership behaviors. The Gestalt perspective of the whole being greater than the sum of its parts is the essence of being strategic. To gain a better appreciation of the "whole" and hence to gain better strategic appreciation is, in Gestalt terms, accomplished through awareness of present realities. Awareness as focal in Gestalt theory is in line with the importance of awareness to savvy. Savvy's roots could be considered grounded in a Gestalt perspective.

To have greater savvy you need to know yourself. Self-awareness, though, is an enigma. Don't we naturally know ourselves better than anyone? Actually, we do not, unless we work at it. We can be oblivious to certain aspects of our personality, behavior, and capability; we can have blind spots. Blind spots pose a potential threat, especially when others see things about us and we do not. Savvy leaders work hard to uncover blind spots. Blind spots are natural and dynamic; we will always have them and they are ever-changing. That being said, they need to be addressed, meaning there needs to be a process created to uncover and deal with them on an ongoing basis. Feedback is viewed as a primary means of uncovering and addressing your blind spots. As such it is a tool that will be highlighted later in this chapter.

Savvy also includes having an awareness of how others perceive you, of your image. Image needs your direct attention and management. Think of yourself as a publicist and your image as your most important client. As a savvy leader, you need a working knowledge of how others see you. You also need to put forth a concerted effort to address your image impediments. Feedback is a means for understanding how others see you and can direct you in dealing with image impediments. This feedback can come to you directly as something told to you by someone or written about you in perhaps a performance evaluation. It can come from various assessment tools that target broad or specific aspects of your personality, values, style, or leadership. It can come from you. You can provide yourself with feedback by better attuning to and understanding your behavior as well as the behavior of others. As such, feedback is a self- and other-empathy tool. Goleman's emotional intelligence theory (called attention to in the chapter on leadership and the brain) identifies self- and other-awareness as a key factor in our effectiveness and success. Emotional intelligence theory highlights and supports the importance of awareness and provides a critical savvy perspective.[9]

To negotiate organizational politics, you need cultural awareness. Cultural awareness is knowledge of what is valued, regarded, and taboo in the arenas you operate within. As a savvy leader you should have an intimate understanding of all cultures you are affected by, from the cultures of your customer groups to your company's operating culture, to the location-specific cultures of various work groups. In Peter's case, his Euro-based plant may have certain cultural nuances different from its sister plants in Asia and the United States. His overall company has a core culture that he needs to be aligned with. His key customer groups reflect different cultural values. In addition to giving attention to the differences between groups, Peter would benefit from looking for commonalities as well. That being said, Peter's low score on *culturally oriented* is something for him to flag. We saw previously how it is already hampering his peer relationships. In the context of his savvy it becomes all the more developmentally important. In Chapter 3, Peter was asked to begin a cultural discovery journal. This is a good start and support for Peter to begin to better develop the trait *culturally oriented*.

Feedback and Feedforward

Two communication tools can help develop greater self-awareness, image awareness, and cultural awareness. Those communication skills are feedforwards and feedback. A feedforward helps create more accurate perceptions in others of what we are saying and doing. It helps us promote a more positive image of ourselves. Feedback helps us become more aware of the image we project. Feedback involves receiving data and information as well as the perspectives of others, how they experience and see things. Through this knowledge, we can come to better understand ourselves, our impact, and the world around us.

Feedback: Savvy's Lifeline

Feedback is knowledge through which we can deepen our awareness. It is a means for providing accurate views of self, image, and the cultures you interact within. Information is power and what you don't want is others having more information than you. Worse still is others having more accurate and realistic information than you. The information focused on in this context is not about the work itself but about the work culture and climate, about those who have the power, and, most importantly, how you are regarded at any given moment. Feedback is our primary tool for this type of information accuracy.

Feedback can take the form of observation. We can look at and listen to what is going on around us and begin to organize observations into data, facts, and assumptions. When speaking, we can scan the room for nonverbal feedback, what the body language and facial expressions of an audience tell us. Fact: You observe that three of the four people in your audience fell asleep. It's not a good sign, but there could be several reasons, among them that it is a 7:00 a.m. Monday meeting. You simply note the information for now. Assumption: Several people did not show up for the meeting because they don't respect you. This could be true, or the meeting could have been scheduled at a bad time, making it difficult for them to attend. When making observations, it is important to separate out facts from assumptions and test our assumptions to make sure they are accurate.

Another form of feedback comes from formal measures like performance evaluations and leadership assessments, such as a Myers-Briggs Type Indicator or 360 Evaluation. Formal tests of this nature give us data about our leadership style and about how others experience us. Employee or customer surveys would also be considered a formal measure. Additionally, individuals can provide us with direct and indirect feedback in the form of statements about us, the work, or the workplace. Feedback can be expressed to us directly from a source, or comments can come to us indirectly, relayed through someone, or by others' demeanor when in their presence.

There is an art to receiving feedback, being open to it, and then dealing with and interpreting it, especially when it is about the problematic.

Some of us ignore or dismiss feedback. From now on, realize that every time you dismiss feedback it is like destroying something of value. Reframe it this way. Envision an object that is precious to you, something that would be hard to replace. The next time you turn away from feedback, imagine that object has just been taken from you. As difficult as it is to hear unfavorable information about you or your standing, it reveals something that needs to be attended to. In fact, the more grim the feedback, the more valuable it is to you.

It is also important to note that while feedback is not always accurate or may not mean literally what it states, it always does mean something. It takes a good investigator to sort through feedback and get to the bottom of its true meaning. Whenever I think of feedback I think of the time I was teaching and a student wrote something on an instructor evaluation that shocked me. I was a relatively new professor. I loved teaching and enjoyed solid relationships with most of my students. At the end of every semester after grades were turned in, we were handed the famed green envelope. In it were evaluations from our students, hundreds of pages of comments and ratings. It was a lot of data to sort through. On this particular day, I was reading the comments and there it was, "She was the biggest disappointment of my life." Well, that wasn't very nice, I thought. I was shocked, really. I kept on reading, page by page, and most of the other evaluations were fine. Now I began to get annoyed: is this person serious, seeing me as her biggest disappointment? Then I took a deep breath and began to think. I decided that, logically speaking, since I did not recall any incidents during the semester something else was at work here.

To make a very long story short I got to the point of acceptance, that I had done something that required further scrutiny. This is what can happen with feedback, especially difficult feedback. It is hard to process at first blush. When it is extreme, there is a tendency to want to dismiss it altogether. I examined this student's feedback next to other less harsh but still critical statements. I talked the feedback over with a colleague who knew me well. The conclusion reached was that my friendly style may be confusing to some. I adjusted my manner, shifting style to the behavior **grounded** in order to add a stabilizing element to my engaging postures. At the end of the following semester the negative comments went away and stayed away. I was able to remain engaging, but I added an element of caution to it. Issues continued to arise from time to time, but through greater awareness they were addressed as they occurred.

There are two morals to this story. The first is that feedback should not be treated as literal; meanings must be interpreted or inferred from the feedback. The second is that knee-jerk reactions to tough feedback are normal. You can move through them and get to a place of reconciliation. What you do from there will make all the difference.

The thing to remember is that if you do not reconcile the feedback, the negative information about you will still be out there. As long as you ignore or cannot accept feedback, valuable information about you will be in others' hands. Think of it this way. When you see yourself on a video or hear yourself on tape, you almost always notice things that you didn't realize before, or you may find it hard to believe that you sound, look, or come across in certain ways. Without the vantage point of looking directly at yourself, you can be blind to certain aspects of your behavior. Others have the opportunity for direct observation all the time. Fortunately for us, a portion of the time others are preoccupied with their own issues and are not attending closely to us. When we are under their direct scrutiny, however, they have valuable information about us. The key is to be privy to that information. Feedback is the way to do that.

Deborrah Himsel, author and leadership expert, wrote a book about an unorthodox leader. That leader is the fictitious television character mafia leader Tony Soprano. In a provocative and humorous analysis, Soprano's leadership qualities were examined. One quality was his ability to deal with feedback. Tony actually received high feedback marks for his willingness to ask for it directly, in Himsel's words, "to his face." This is not such an easy thing to do. Himsel has this to say about feedback:

- Feedback is not something to fear; reframe it from potentially hurtful to necessary.
- If you don't like it, you do have the option of disagreeing with it.
- People's intentions are usually good, meaning they are trying to protect or help you.
- Be proactive in going after the feedback rather than being a source of gossip.
- Don't personalize feedback. In Himsel's words, "don't shoot the messenger." Maintain your composure and listen.[10]

This is sound advice from Himsel, especially the part about maintaining your cool. Feedback cuts directly to our self-esteem. The question you have to ask yourself is: do I want to be told I am great, or do I want to know how to become great? Consider adopting a process for making feedback a regular part of your life. It needs to become second nature to you for all the good it has to offer. Lastly, when reflecting on the feedback you receive, look for true meaning. Get below the surface to the heart of messages.

Feedback is a high-level tool that requires supplemental support from tools you are already familiar with, tools that can structure and aid how you solicit and evaluate feedback. Referring again to Madison and Peter, how can they embrace this high-level tool? What more straightforward tools can help them?

To begin with, they could each initiate a feedback log. For Madison, a structured log would also aid her methodical development, a left brain style shift. For Peter, it would ground him in a preferred style for what will be a more challenging pursuit. To make such a log, list feedback sources, page by page, leaving ample space to record the feedback. Create a key indicating whether the feedback was from an observation, from formal assessments, or from direct or indirect dialogue. If any assumptions are made, highlight them and look for ways to test your assumptions. Set a goal of having to acquire a specific number of feedback points over the course of a month, pushing yourself to seek feedback.

In addition to structured logs, Madison and Peter could set up unstructured journals to write about their experiences as they seek out and process feedback. They could each use a cue to prompt them to solicit feedback, something tangible like a key chain that they carry with them with some meaningful symbol. Peter could carry a key chain with the letter "P" for perception. Madison could set her planner with a reminder alert to solicit feedback. Deep breathing could help them as it did me when they hear something unnerving.

One could use chaining to structure successive steps to ask for more and more intensive feedback. You could begin by going to someone close to you, someone you trust, and simply asking a direct question: "What did you think of how I handled the questions at the meeting yesterday?" When you move to more intensive feedback, be sure to give the person you are asking the reasons you need their input. For example, you could say: "Maria, I've been trying to work on being less abrupt and listening more. When we were talking yesterday about the problems you are having with my team, were you able to tell me everything you needed to? What could I do better next time, or how can we structure the conversation better?" In the latter example you told the person why you needed her input. You asked the question in a way that allowed her to talk about her experience rather than to talk about you personally, which is sometimes difficult for people. You also gave her an opportunity to collaborate with you on next time.

Just as you use feedback to better know yourself, feedback can also be used to better know the cultures around you. To be more attuned to cultures, look for feedback that will give you answers to the following questions:

- Who has the power and why?
- What is rewarded and why?
- What is respected and why?
- What does the work environment or setting reveal about the culture?
- How do the people dress, act, and relate to one another?

- What is celebrated and what form do celebrations take?
- What kind of information is displayed and available?
- What constitutes a mistake, failure, or blunder?
- How are mistakes, failures, and blunders dealt with?

Gaining greater awareness through feedback will put Madison and Peter on more solid political ground. For Madison, it will also enable her to have a better sense for subtlety and timing. For Peter, subtlety and his ability to assimilate will be advanced.

Feedforward: Upfront Impressions

A feedforward is information you provide that prepares others for what you are about to say. It can serve a number of purposes, such as to open the lines of communication, which is referred to as phatic communication. Phatic communication is that which sets a mood, or a social nicety. A feedforward can also express an expectation. Starting a speech by saying, "We have an opportunity at this session to come together, learn from each other, and open the door to better working relationships," is an example of how a feedforward message passes on an expectation. A feedforward also can provide a disclaimer.[11] For example, in a conversation with your boss you might start by saying, "I've got the report here and while we're not there yet, we are off to a solid start." This upfront message alerts your boss that the work is in progress and will be delivered in great shape. A feedforward can further serve to establish your role in a given situation. Consider: "We've all worked together for a long time on many projects and issues, but as team leader on this project, I need to know where each of you is on this matter that's causing us such difficulty." In this example, your message requests that people reply to you as the leader, not to you as a colleague. Feedforward messages enable you to get off on a positive note, to influence perceptions, circumvent misunderstandings at the outset, and to be seen as more responsible overall. In using this skill you are doing proactive work on your image.

Madison and Peter can both benefit from this tool. Since it is a new communication tool for them they should start slowly, using a chaining paradigm. They can start with someone they know well and are comfortable with to practice, and as they feel successful with it they can add on a new person or situation. Start with a friend or family member, then move to someone you know well at work, then to the member of your team with whom you are most comfortable, and so on.

A Mentor for Peter

Peter is still left with the challenge of becoming more networking and coalition-building. Peter is socially apprehensive. He can do the work and relates well to those who work for him and his bosses. Networking and coalition-building, however, are social conundrums for Peter. A mentor could serve as his bridge to greater savvy as well as providing a comfortable feedback source. Peter needs to be brought along socially by someone he trusts and is at ease with, someone more senior and established who could shepherd him in this process while also enabling Peter to practice with feedback and feedforwards. Below is a summary showing Peter's style shift.

Peter's SAVVY Style Shift Summary

High scores: *Astute, diplomatic, timely*

Alter-brain depth targets: *Subtle, culturally oriented, assimilating, networking, coalition-building*

Tools: Understand SMEs Brandon and Seldman and Badaracco's savvy perspectives, Himsel's feedback perspective, and Goleman's perspective on awareness, and attend a seminar on perception. Develop feedback skill with the help of a feedback log and journal, cuing, and deep breathing. Use chaining to assist with feedforward. Get a mentor.

Savvy as Right- and Left-Brain Enhancing

Developing better savvy has immeasurable benefits. Like its partner Plus Factor **resilient**, through the development of **savvy**, multiple right and left brain behaviors are enhanced. Think of Madison a year from now adding subtlety and timing to her communications. Imagine her also as mindful of promoting herself and her team and building important coalitions at work. Think of Peter as less blunt, working to fit into a group and understand and leverage its norms and values. Imagine him networking and coming together with others who share a common cause. Picture both Peter and Madison making use of feedback and becoming more aware and spot-on in how they see things. Madison's savvy will help her to better gauge how and when to use her innovative skill and when to shift her style to the more structured and grounded. Peter's savvy will reinforce his right brain engaging skill as well as his left brain assertive gaps with respect to his peer group.

Look at the ways savvy is right- and left-brain enhancing overall. Through deeper awareness of your circumstance and personal position, you will be able to land on more astute strategic alternatives. Having the full understanding of the organization's existing culture and being more timely, assimilative, and subtle in how you approach reinvention can help with your transformational leadership. As you are more visible and keyed in, others will experience you as more grounded. Your expressive and engaging skills also will take on new dimension as you communicate more tactfully. Your ability to engage is also bolstered through having a support system in place, the result of your networking and coalition-building. **Savvy** is in many ways the most taxing behavior to develop; that which derives the utmost benefit usually is. How does that saying go, "saved the best for last"?

Having covered the best and the last of the ten guiding behaviors, we come to the book's final chapter. A roadmap to your right brain and left brain breadth and depth is offered as we move from our four cases to how you personally can apply the book's knowledge to your own development.

CHAPTER 7

THE ROADMAP: GETTING TO BREADTH AND DEPTH

Life is like a ten speed bike. Most of us have gears we never use.

—*Charles Schulz*

Now is your opportunity for accessing all of your leadership gears through the creation of a right brain / left brain development plan. Given what you have learned about leadership, about behavioral preferences and the value of extending beyond them, the question is: are you ready to shift your style for greater breadth and depth? I was on a plane recently, reading the *Wall Street Journal*. There on the front page of the second section was a headline, "This is your brain on the job." The article showed hi-tech images of the brains of leaders. At Arizona State University, research was underway to "plot a map of a leader's brain." The study's hypothesis was that leaders, especially visionaries, use their brains differently from others. The hope was to use this information as an enrichment tool for all leaders. The article pointed to the growing interest in how neuroscience can inform organizational development.[1] The Right Brain / Left Brain Leadership Model affords the opportunity to put your newfound multidisciplinary knowledge to work for you, blending current perspectives from neuroscience and organizational and personal development toward more substantive next-level leadership.

This final chapter will begin with a right brain / left brain recap naming ten leadership imperatives. Next, it will detail a four-step development plan. The plan's steps equate to the four key leadership processes defined at the book's outset: visioning, operationalizing, implementing, and declaring. You will be taken through an assessment process to help you decide on alter-brain development targets and plot out a means to reach them. You will be shown a way to review your progress and be presented with an organized listing of development resources. The book will conclude by sharing parting inspirations.

Right Brain/Left Brain Recap: Ten Leadership Imperatives

The Right Brain / Left Brain Leadership Model with its counter-intuitive approach challenges you to push beyond your usual skill sets. It provides ten guiding behaviors and 100 behavioral nuances to help you extend yourself. Your primary extension process is twofold: making a style shift from right to left and left to right, which is your means for accessing greater leadership breadth, and developing new traits within a given behavior, for greater depth. Numerous and varied tools assist this alter-brain approach.

You are about to create a personalized development plan. As you build your plan, keep in mind the key elements of the right brain / left brain perspective. These ten imperatives crystallize what the Right Brain / Left Brain Leadership Model is all about.

1. **Orient your leadership from right to left.** This counter-intuitive approach begins by looking out at possibilities. The leader's Line of SITE and its behaviors—**strategic**, **innovative**, **transformational**, and **engaging**—conceptualize what is possible and get you the buy-in needed from those around you to get you there. The leader's MEGA Mind and its behaviors—**methodical**, **expressive**, **grounded**, and **assertive**—make possibilities a reality. The Plus Factors—**resilient** and **savvy**—are ever-present adjuncts to bolster and secure your overall effectiveness.

2. **Work differently, not harder.** Recognize your preferences. Know when they work in your favor and when they don't. Be willing and able to push beyond them for the greater impact you need, especially when challenged.

3. **When stuck in a preference, shift style.** When stuck in your left brain preferences, shift style through discovery and reflection. When stuck in your right brain preferences, shift style through discipline and rehearsal. When stuck altogether, ground yourself in your preference and reach across the model or down into a behavior's traits for the alter-brain breadth or depth you need.

4. **Avoid the quick fix.** When challenged, always ask yourself: what do I ultimately want to accomplish? Take a broader, more proactive view. Resist the tendency to treat the immediate issue and look instead for solutions that get to root causes.

5. **Manage your energy throughout the day.** Move, hydrate, and breathe. Promote circulation and mitigate muscle tension with three simple but effective remedies: use movement (walking, shifting seat position, and light stretching), drink plenty of water, and remember to periodically take slow deep breaths.

6. **Create dynamic interplays.** Through ongoing shifting, in this case, shifting back and forth between right and left brain behaviors, one generates the

dynamic interplays necessary for greater forward momentum and success. If you are great at right brain engaging, shift mindset to the assertive left and ask yourself this: "I know they know I value them, but do they know I mean business?" If you are assertive, shift mindset to the transformational right and ask yourself this: "I know they are compliant, but are they my ambassadors?" and so on.

7. **Promote synergies.** Your brain thrives on them, so too should you. A synergy is any combined effort that nets a greater result. The saying "two heads are better than one" comes to mind. Look for more ways that you and those you interact with can work collaboratively, share knowledge and information, and pool resources.

8. **Go natural.** If you want to improve your perspective, improve your environment. Take a break, get away, and commune with nature. As you venture into your natural environment, go the extra step to consider what more you can do personally to protect it.

9. **Build a library on leadership, not book-of-the-month picks.** There are countless resources on all aspects of leading. Use them. Organize your thinking around the ten guiding behaviors and integrate into them the many perspectives presented in this book, together with other perspectives that you have and will continue to discover. That is how to truly get to breadth and depth.

10. **Make feedback your new best friend.** Embrace it, listen to it, respect it, and keep it close at all times.

Your Plan: A Return to the Four Key Processes

The Right Brain / Left Brain Leadership Model identifies four key processes leaders use in their work. They are visioning, operationalizing, implementing, and declaring. To refresh our understanding: leaders conceptualize their work around a mission and direction, which is their visioning. Leaders operationalize their work by developing plans and allocating resources. Leaders implement their operational plans by driving certain actions. Leaders make declarations based on a culling of best practices and by identifying areas for improvement and change.

Applying these four processes to any development plan, you will see that visioning equates to our aspirations, gaining an understanding of where we are relative to where we would like to be. Visioning relies heavily on feedback and has as its end result the identification of deliberate development targets, right brain / left brain style shifts that will have the greatest impact on your success. Operationalizing equates to your methodology, your ways and means of addressing these growth targets. It includes specifying objectives (the purpose you will achieve through attention to a given target), success measures (indicators that you have in fact met your objectives), time frames (how long you anticipate it will take to address a target), and resources (tools that will facilitate progress). Implementing includes specific steps or actions you will take, along with how you will hold yourself accountable to complete the set actions. Declaring is a review process and includes how you evaluate progress, learn from it, and decide on next steps.

The full development plan will be shown in this chapter with examples using Angela's case. Blank worksheets for each section of the plan are found in the book's appendix, and electronic copies may be accessed at www.leadlifeinstitute.com. You may use these to complete your own development plan following the steps below.

Steps in Your Development Plan

1. Visioning narrative
2. Sponsor feedback
3. Feedback summary
4. Visioning summary
5. Rating yourself
6. Operationalizing summary
7. Implementation design
8. Declaring progress

Visioning: Angela's Aspirations

Visioning begins with a narrative reflection in which you capture your leadership aspirations concerning your organization's culture, teams, individuals, and yourself. Your visioning time frame should be one year. One year from now, if you could be better in each of those areas, what would "better" look like? Angela's visioning narrative below illustrates how it is done.

Worksheet 1 — Visioning Narrative *(completed by Angela)*

Write a short statement next to each heading describing how, within one year from now, you envision leading your organization's cultural development and alignment, your team's effectiveness, the performance development of key individuals, and how you as an overall leader would like to be functioning.

Cultures — *I'll be aligning my team better with the overall culture of the organization, helping to evolve their mindset to one of collaboration and* *innovation so that they will work better across the organization and be open to new ways of doing things.*

Teams — *I'll be moving them from a group of collegial individual contributors to real collaborators, trusting in and relying on each other in all aspects of our work.*

Individuals — *I'll be giving more direct feedback to my direct reports on ways I need them to change and grow, rather than praising them and hoping that will motivate them to change.*

Self — *I'll be more able to deal with conflict and come across as being more assertive.*

The second aspect of your visioning involves feedback. You would begin by identifying feedback sources, which will be both formal and informal. Formal feedback sources include assessments, surveys, evaluations, and performance data. Informal feedback sources include observations you make, what you glean from situations, conversations, or interactions, and what is directly told to you by others in conversation.

Formal feedback should provide foundational information concerning your day-to-day behavioral style and approaches. It should also help you understand how you are viewed by others throughout the organization. Sources such as the MBTI (Myers-Briggs Type Indicator) and HPI (Hogan Personality Inventory) provide general measures of style and preferences. The FIRO-B (Fundamental Interpersonal Relations Orientation – Behavior) is an assessment that helps you understand your interpersonal behavior. As such it gives you additional insights into your actions and reactions. Another type of assessment, 360 Evaluations, solicit feedback from bosses, peers, direct reports, and customers, showing how you are viewed by the various groups you interface with. You rate yourself as well so that you can compare others' ratings to how you see yourself.

The assessments described thus far give you insights into your everyday leadership style. You should also seek to understand your effectiveness over time and when challenged. In addition, expand your awareness from the vantage point of external perspectives, perspectives of those outside of your own organization.

A leadership assimilation is a facilitated discussion between you and your immediate team that is organized around a set of questions about who you are, how you lead, and what your goals and intents are. It furnishes a snapshot of how your work and style has been experienced over a prescribed period of time. Different from a 360 Evaluation, leadership assimilations offer you and your team a face-to-face dialoguing mechanism. Typically conducted after six months or so in a position, a leadership assimilation is a structured, facilitated experience where the team is asked questions about your adjustment and effectiveness. The team can also ask questions of you and make recommendations or suggestions concerning what they need from you. Assimilations are a valuable gauge for how your team sees you. They afford the opportunity for better alignment and allow you to correct misimpressions.

When we are challenged our reactions are put to a test. Challenging times are pivotal times because our behavior under stress is in many ways more important to leading than how we act day in and day out. More targeted assessments are available to help us gain a deeper view of our reactions under pressure. The HDS (Hogan Development Survey) is one such tool. It provides insight into behavioral drawbacks, those that can potentially compromise your effectiveness, especially when under stress.

Professional seminars bring you together with subject matter experts and with leaders from different organizations and industries. They enable you to learn about leadership with new colleagues outside of your present circumstance. Distanced from your work environment, you can have fresh conversations while also viewing your capability from the perspective of a different audience.

Finally, you should be prepared to solicit formal feedback from what is referred to here as a sponsor. The word "sponsor" is loosely defined to mean any individual you believe to have a relevant perspective on your development status. It can be a boss, human resources person, colleague, friend, family member, or customer who is willing to complete a short status report illustrated in the following example. Angela solicited sponsor feedback from her boss and provided the following instructions; you will use Worksheet 2 and do something similar: "I am in the process of creating a leadership development plan. Your feedback is a greatly valued part of my learning process. If you could please take a moment to answer the following questions and e-mail the completed form to me within a week, it would be greatly appreciated."

Worksheet 2 — Sponsor Feedback *(completed by Angela's boss)*

Ask an individual whom you believe has a relevant perspective on your development status to complete the following (a boss, human resources person, colleague, friend, family member, or customer).

1. Comment on this leader's understanding of and alignment with the organization's culture, mission, and current goals. Note specific strengths and needs. *Angela is well aligned with what we are all about and what we need to accomplish. She is a solid thinker and communicator. She works* *hard and is a great model for her team. She needs to expect more from her people and push them harder.*

2. Comment on this leader's communication strengths and needs.
Angela is a great speaker and writer. She is diplomatic and makes sure her team has the information they need. She is very good at motivating through what she says and how she says it. She is soft though on delivering tough messages.

3. Comment on this individual's leadership style, strengths, and opportunities for development. *Angela is a good leader overall, mostly because she cares and has a vested interest in others. Her style is to support and engage. She is less likely to be as assertive as a situation may require. She needs to know when to stop the discussions and make overt demands.*

4. Comment on this individual's ability to influence up, down, and across the organization. *Angela is respected throughout the organization. She deals well up, down, and across except for needing to expect more from her team.*

5. Comment on this individual's interpersonal skills and relationships. *Very good overall.*

6. Note any additional feedback you think would be helpful at this time. *Nothing else comes to mind at this time.*

Up-to-date personal performance data is a key feedback element. You should also be thinking of current challenges and opportunities for your team or organization. Employee and customer surveys can be useful supplements in illuminating issues and opportunities. When your feedback is all gathered, it will be culled into a summary. The feedback summary is provided on Worksheet 3 and includes the following:

Worksheet 3 — Feedback Summary *(completed by Angela)*
Record insights and information from all current and indirect feedback sources as follows:

Formal assessment results or highlights — *No formal assessments were completed this time, but looking back at what was in my file from a year or so ago shows that I am high on interpersonal qualities and lower on driving and challenging.*

Insights from any courses or seminars attended — *Saw that many leaders have trouble with confrontation for different reasons. For me it seems to keep coming back to wanting to be thought of as a good boss, and good means fair, understanding, and likeable. I can keep those qualities and add more, like being serious, direct, and persistent—it doesn't have to be an either/or.*

Performance evaluation data (note areas where you are on track versus at risk) — *Our team is at risk for hitting stretch targets.*

Noteworthy current organizational issues, circumstances, or opportunities — *Many new-customer opportunities exist due to the company's recent expanded capability.*

Highlights from Sponsor Feedback — *I need to get tougher in what I expect and how I get results.*

Informal feedback insights (what you are hearing or noticing that is particularly relevant) — *The organization overall seems taxed and stressed, which may hamper how we are able to tap into our opportunities. Though my team seems oppositional at times, they do want to succeed and seem to trust me.*

Using what you learned from your visioning narrative, sponsor feedback, and feedback summary, you can now rate yourself on our ten guiding behaviors. The circle charts used throughout the book to rate Angela, Ken, Madison, and Peter will be your means to do so. Blank copies of all the charts are found on Worksheet 4 in the appendix. For each behavior, rate yourself somewhere between low and high on each trait (low is the center point of the circle). Mark the position on the chart and connect the dots. (Traits and their definitions are detailed in Chapters 3–6, if you need to review.)

Having completed the needed feedback and ratings information, you will then complete a visioning summary and ultimately identify specific alter-brain targets. The visioning summary asks you to first identify key challenges, then to record high and low ratings and, finally, to land on three to five alter-brain targets. When choosing targets, don't simply look at your lowest scores. Look at what will have the greatest impact and what will address your challenges. Also consider targets that are attainable. A visioning summary is provided on Worksheet 5 and shown in the following example.

Worksheet 5 — Visioning Summary *(completed by Angela)*

Use your ratings information to identify key challenges, record high and low ratings, and select 3–5 alter-brain targets.

Key Leadership Challenges: Based on your current status, feedback, and circumstance, what are your three key challenges?

1. *To become more assertive*

2. *To hit our targets*

3. *To develop and transform my team*

Right Brain/Left Brain Ratings: Record your high and low ratings.

Ten highest ratings: *Positive, emotionally sound, tolerant, flexible, attuned, incremental, mentoring, open to learning, articulate, persuasive*

Ten lowest ratings: *Ambiguity-seeking, opportunity-conscious, relaxed, clear thinking, physically fit, tenacious, confrontational, courageous, candid, coalition-building*

Alter-Brain Targets: Based on your current feedback and circumstance, identify the 3–5 breadth and/or depth style shifts that would most favorably impact your development. Include the specific traits that you will develop.

1. *Breadth with a style shift from engaging to assertive—tenacious, confrontational, courageous, candid*

2. *Resilient depth—physically fit, relaxed, clear thinking*

3. *Savvy depth—coalition-building*

4. *Transformational depth—Ambiguity-seeking, opportunity-conscious*

The visioning section of this development plan is purposely intensive. Through a more rigorous process of gaining and sorting through feedback and thinking about what would have the most impact on your effectiveness, you will select targets more intentionally, targets that will net you the best possible result. Your next step is to detail the methods you will use to develop the behaviors and traits you selected as growth opportunities.

Operationalizing: Angela's Methods

Operationalizing involves the creation of a detailed map to reach your goals. Objectives, success measures, time frames and resources are identified. Two appendices are included in this book to give you assistance in selecting the most suitable tools for your own development plan. The first support is Tools by Trait, showing for each of the 100 traits which tools you should consider. The second aid is a Leadership Library with suggested readings and a summary description of each to direct you to some of the SMEs who can enhance your behavior and trait development. The aim is for you to begin to use the wide array of leadership books out there as part of an ongoing reference library and to find interrelationships between experts. You will gain the most by growing an integrated knowledge base around the concepts presented in this book, rather than treating information as a one-time exercise. An operationalizing summary detailing one of Angela's targets is presented in the following example, Worksheet 6. You will complete an operationalizing summary for each of your alter-brain targets.

Worksheet 6 — Operationalizing Summary *(for Angela's Target #1)*

Create a detailed plan for each of the alter-brain targets identified on Worksheet 5. Use the Tools by Trait list to help determine which tools to consider for each target. Complete a separate worksheet for each target.

Target: *Shift style from engaging to assertive*

Objective: *Be able to confront difficult situations, be more direct, and be seen as more formidable*

Success measure: *360 Evaluation feedback*

Time frame: *Six months*

Tools: *Cuing, reframing, chaining, SMEs*

Implementing: Angela's Actions and Accountability

Implementing is where two important aspects of your development plan occur. The first is to describe the specific actions you will take, how you will use your tools, and what you must do in order to change your intended behaviors. The second and most crucial dimension of implementation is to describe how you will hold yourself accountable. The term "accountability partner" is used in this section and refers to an individual or planning aid that keeps you on track. Individual accountability partners can be a boss, mentor, colleague, family member, or friend. Angela's implementation design for her target to shift style from engaging to assertive is shown in the following example on Worksheet 7.

Worksheet 7 — Implementation Design *(for Angela's Target #1)*

Describe how you will operationalize the development plan (Worksheet 6) and how you will hold yourself accountable. Complete a separate worksheet for each target.

Target: *Shift style from engaging to assertive*

Actions:

1. Select a cue, a symbol that I can have with me at all times to remind me to be tougher. Back this cue up with a second cue, a visual reminder in my office, a picture or poster that I can associate with strength and perseverance. Have a third cue, an inspirational quote, as my new computer and BlackBerry screen saver. Look for new quotes once a month.

2. Reframe my thinking about leadership, that strong is as important as likeable because strong will actually keep my team safe—will ensure that they keep their jobs and income. Create a new written platform to reflect an enhancement to how I see leadership and effectiveness, that strong and direct keeps us safe.

3. Hold one meeting a week with a different member of my team to give them direct feedback about their effectiveness and movement from where they are now to where they need to be. Start with my most effective person (the easiest one to talk with) and proceed from there.

4. Read two books with specific information on accountability and delivering tough messages.

Accountability partners:

1. Put a reminder on my planner for the end of every week to reflect on my application of the three cues I am putting into effect.

2. Ask Alan (assertive colleague) if he would have lunch with me once a month for the next three months to talk about my progress and hold me to my plan.

3. Put a reminder in my planner to be sure I am holding these meetings.

4. Tell my team I will be reading two books that will have value for our work and that I am going to provide them all with a book report when I'm done with each. Assign one of them to check in with me in a month for a date for the first report.

Date set for progress review: *Three months from today*

Implementation planning is important for obvious reasons. You can create a great set of actions, but if you fail to put them into effect, the value is lost. It is easy to get distracted by other demands and pressures and let development slip. For that reason, keep your overall targets simple and realistic. Taking on less and seeing the actions through is of far greater value than an intricate but improbable plan.

Consider also the nature of some of Angela's actions. Her first action, to create three cues, is important because she is attacking the problem with the same assertiveness she is trying to develop in herself. She is becoming more tenacious not just as a result of the tool she chose, but by virtue of how she is implementing the tool. She has cues coming at her from three sources and in three very different ways, with a symbol she will carry, a visual on her wall, and constant reminders electronically. In addition, having to update her quote monthly, she will better internalize her changes through repetition and novel messages. Her cues, her newly created description of leadership, and her book reports all have the added benefit of involving her team. She is coaching them in an indirect but powerful way to adopt what she is learning.

Lastly, her implementation plans leverage her existing strengths in the behaviors **expressive** and **engaging** to develop her lesser assertive side. Strengths used to mitigate weaknesses afford greater assurance that you will be successful.

Declaring: Angela's Progress

In the final phase of your plan, schedule a point in the near future to review progress, reflect on your insights, and determine where to go from here. Depending on your plan, reviews should occur anywhere from monthly to quarterly. You may want to review a particularly challenging target sooner or more frequently than those where you seem to be making good headway. Some suggested questions for declaring progress are shared in the following example, Worksheet 8.

Worksheet 8 — Declaring Progress *(for Angela's Target #1)*

Review your progress on developing each identified target. Reflect on your insights and determine where to go from here.

Target: *Shift style from engaging to assertive*

Reflections:

What have you accomplished relative to your development plan? *I am having more open and difficult conversations with my direct reports and I am seen as stronger.*

What tools, resources, processes worked particularly well and why? *The cues, using writing and presenting to engage new concepts (things I am already good at), and the accountability measures, especially the one-on-ones with Alan to push me to do what I said I would. The reason these methods in particular were so helpful was because they played on my strengths and preferences to address weaknesses. I was able to use techniques within my comfort zone to push behavior out of that zone.*

What haven't you been able to accomplish? *I am still struggling with confrontation. I have done it to a small degree, more than in the past, but I see many missed opportunities.*

Why is this so? *I am not sure I have targeted it as directly as I need to. I need to look for specific issues or situations that require confrontation and one at a time get a plan in place to go after them.*

Course corrections and next steps: *Keep doing what I am doing and target two confrontations this month. Ask Alan to mentor me on how to approach the two situations.*

Declaring helped validate several aspects of Angela's success while showing where her plan needed to be added to and bolstered. This was an initial review of progress for one target. In addition, she will be looking for feedback in the coming months from her 360 Evaluation in order to assess her effectiveness more fully. Through this kind of diligent follow up, you will be more likely to stick to your development commitments.

Your development plan now complete; you are poised to take your leadership to the next level.

Parting Inspirations

It is a Friday afternoon at about 5:30. I just completed a call with a client and am putting the final touches on this book. It is a fitting time to be wrapping up a lengthy project, with a weekend ahead. Reflecting on the entire writing experience, many things come to mind. What stands out most at the moment is the value I have garnered from ongoing work with clients, especially in tandem with this writing process. The leaders I am so very privileged to work with on their respective style shifts have at every juncture informed and validated the book's perspective. More will be said in the book's acknowledgments, but for now I am going to take a deep breath, hold this touching thought, and close by shifting not your style but your attention from my voice to the voices of ten inspirational individuals.

> To laugh often and much; to win the respect of intelligent people and the affection of children; to earn the appreciation of honest critics; to find the best in others; to leave the world a bit better. This is to have succeeded.
>
> —*Bessie Anderson Stanley*

> Change your thoughts and you change your world.
>
> —*Norman Vincent Peale*

> All serious daring starts from within.
>
> —*Eudora Wetly*

> You cannot dream yourself into a character; you must hammer and forge yourself one.
>
> —*James A. Froude*

> Luck is a matter of preparation meeting opportunity.
>
> —*Oprah Winfrey*

> Diamonds are nothing more than coal that stuck to their jobs.
>
> —*Malcolm Stevenson Forbes*

> A positive attitude may not solve all your problems, but it will annoy enough people to make it worth the effort.
>
> —*Herm Albright*

Leadership and learning go hand in hand.

—John F. Kennedy

There is nothing like returning to a place that remains unchanged to find the ways in which you yourself have altered.

—Nelson Mandela

Go confidently in the direction of your dreams. Live the life you've always imagined.

—Henry David Thoreau

Thank you for letting me be part of your leadership dreams.

ACKNOWLEDGMENTS

It is difficult for a writer to admit being without words, but that is precisely the case when I try and express what the project of writing this book has meant to me. An initiative such as this pushes and helps us grow in every way imaginable. For the experience itself, the book deserves first recognition.

Dr. Christopher Stout is an amazing individual who comes to mind next. I met Chris on a project we were working on together many years ago. I tease him that the only explanation for Chris being able to accomplish what he does is that he must be an identical triplet, his siblings behind the scenes and he the front-guy. One of his involvements is as editor of a contemporary psychology series. I applied to write a book for the series and *Right Brain/Left Brain Leadership* was on its way. Chris has given his total support. His manner of interaction and scholarship is unsurpassed. Heartfelt thanks to Chris as well as to my publisher, Greenwood Publishing Group, especially Debbie Carvalko for her strategic guidance, and to Elizabeth Claeys for her detailed direction.

The book's dedication mentions three individuals. My husband, Jean-Pierre, is a genuinely great leader. His business integrity in what can be ruthless environments has always set him apart. His unyielding refusal to play games is more than respectable. How he consistently chooses the greater good over his own is what makes him particularly admirable. I thank him for serving as my model for grounded and savvy leadership. I also thank him for his personal support and patience during this entire project. I cherish the times he brought his work into the study to be quietly close by while I wrote. Jerri Frantzve, who wrote the book's foreword, is my friend and business partner. She is my alter-brain mentor and I am hers. Learning to work together, to integrate strengths, and to respect each other's differences has been life-changing. Her innovative wisdom drives the projects we work on together through their pivotal moments. Outcomes have all been "the best." My mom, Rosemarie, is amazing. She continues to run circles around the rest of us with what seems to be never-ending energy. She loves to laugh and reminds us always what's really important. I thank her for her resilient inspiration: to, in her words, "toughen up!" Also a talented writer, she taught me to "keep it crisp." The consummate tennis player, she continuously advises me on and off the court that "if you don't want the ball to hit you in the face, get ready or get out of the way."

Regarding our daughters, Patricia and Yasmine, it is moving to be a part of their growth as leaders and to watch them come into their own. We are so very proud of what they have accomplished, and I am grateful to see through their eyes what up and coming leaders face.

My sister Linda's innovative gift has been there to remind me when "it doesn't always have to be symmetrical," and my brother Buddy and father Tony's methodical sense is there to tell me when it does. My step-mother Bernice is there to remind us what engaging looks like, and my sister-in-law Carol's inner strength is an inspiration to us all. We have amazing young people in our family whose perspectives are precious gifts. Nikki is our environmentalist, Sarah our unconventional breath of fresh air, and Gina our change agent, while Sam's magnanimous spirit fuels our souls.

My lifelong friends Sue Spinella and Valerie Gerardi have always been there and ultimately kept me true to course. My mom, Aunt Laura, and Aunt Toni, along with my siblings, cousins, and uncles are a tribute to teamwork. My remarkable puppies, Max and Lilly, are such great rejuve-nators I was inclined to put pet therapy in as a support tool. The members of my Swiss family, though far away, are never far from thought, and they are truly appreciated for their genuineness, love, and support.

In keeping with the theme of resilience, there are four noteworthy women to acknowledge: my sister-in-law Susi Décosterd, and friends and colleagues Jessica Tonna, Shari Simon, and Holli Beckwith. Thanks to them for continuing to inform my wellness and spiritual perspective and for the special gift of knowing them.

The professional journey that ultimately resulted in this work began in the field of psychology. The University of Hartford is where I learned the basics of the book's many tools and perspectives. From Julian Streitfeld and James Matthews I learned behavioral and cognitive approaches, from Robert Leve I became hooked on development, and from Alan Schiffer

I learned the affective approaches, in particular the Gestalt perspective on awareness and the "whole."

I then studied at and worked for the University of Oklahoma's Advanced Programs at Fort Sill, serving the U.S. military. This experience was important in coming to know the formidable perspective and culture of esteemed military leaders. While at the university I studied educational psychology, keying in on the role of learning in behavior change. Upon graduation I went to work for the Jim Taliaferro Community Mental Health Center in my first leadership assignment. Under the mentoring of Dr. Royce Means, Dr. Edith King, Georgia Wykoff, and Dr. Rosa Lee Brown, I began to apply the principles of psychology and learning to client treatment programs, individual and group therapy, and staff training and development. My first leadership feedback was curious at the time. I was told to slow down and not make any changes for the first month, an alter-brain advice I came to appreciate and adopt.

I relocated back east and continued in the field of psychology, working at Marist and Dutchess Community Colleges, Holy Cross, Anderson School, and the Astor Home for Children. Throughout these clinical and educational assignments I served as a leader, educator, and clinician working with diverse cultural groups, extreme communication and behavioral problems, neurological and health disorders, and severe stress reactions.

I continued to hone a leadership perspective by integrating an understanding of the brain and came to realize the need for dynamic interplay. In critical environments, where extreme and sometimes violent or life-threatening behaviors are commonplace, the balance between the strategic and the tactical, the innovative and the expressive, the grounded and the transformational, and most importantly, the engaging and the assertive, become necessary not just for success, but for survival. Resilient and savvy behaviors were key in averting worker burnout and negotiating the layered political bureaucracies we were engulfed by. Working in this psychologically and sociologically complex milieu, power, perceptions, awareness, and feedback became my focus for staff and clients alike. Dynamic interplay along with these four critical concepts became the foundation for my work with the leaders I later came to serve.

Many individuals supported and mentored my perspectives. I owe special gratitude to Jim Lennon and Carl Denti, who were inspirational bosses and leaders in their own right and went above and beyond the call to mentor. Each with his unique hallmarks of leadership, their combined styles informed the selection of many behavioral traits. Herb Kaplin, our most respected elder, was always there with the guidance needed, and David Sherwood, my personal coach, showed me firsthand the potential unleashed through true awareness. Margaret Gold was my model for leading from the unique gifts of a female perspective. My friends

and colleagues David and Tammy Rosenthal, Pat Lamanna, Mareve Van
Voorhis, Toni Emery, Rita Banner, Sue and John Stern, and Donna Zulch
continue to enrich the lives of all those they touch personally and professionally.

I studied advanced assessment and psychological technique at the
College of New Rochelle and was mentored by an exceptional woman,
Irma Brownfield, who masterfully developed and nurtured intuition in
her students. Jim Magee taught me how to blend and balance the factual
with the intuitive in assessment. Upon completion of a post-master's
certificate, I was invited to teach at New Rochelle's graduate college. In
that experience I learned firsthand about stretching oneself and rising to
a challenge. It was there that I met Jerri Frantzve, my then department
head, who supported that exigent time. I also continued to work as a tenured faculty member at Dutchess Community College and took training
assignments at its Center for Business and Industry, working with various
corporations. My migration to consulting was fully underway.

I consulted for several profit and nonprofit organizations and made the
decision to return to school for a PhD. I attended the Fielding Institute,
through which it became possible to develop and marry eclectic knowledge and expertise in psychology, sociology, education, business, and
organizational development. I thank the Fielding faculty I was so fortunate to have worked with, in particular, David Rehorick for his teachings
in phenomenology, leadership, and research; Annabelle Nelson for her
innovative perspectives, neuro-psych and therapeutic brilliance; Leonard
Baca for his humanistic manner, showing how to engage others in subtle
yet powerful ways; Henry Soper and Marilyn Friemuth for their clinical
stewardship; and Charlie Seashore, Jeremy Shaprio, and Keith Melville
for their consummate sociological and organizational development
wisdom.

I lived and worked as a consultant abroad and then relocated to
Chicago and became a partner at the consulting firm Executive Partners,
Inc. There, owner and founder Rob Oberwise, partner Gene Gerard, and
I collaborated on a training project where we first conceptualized a self-
development trilogy, thinking which later evolved into the book's energy
model. I advanced my work in strategic thinking, attitude setting, and
transformation through Rob and Gene's mentoring.

Wanting to work from a perspective more seated in psychology,
I founded the Lead Life Institute. Anita Augustine, my then mentor, was
instrumental in getting the company off the ground. Anita's organiza-
tional development and leadership expertise is unsurpassed. She is a
great colleague and friend whose counsel is held in the highest regard.
Friends and colleagues Fran Holmstrom, Michael and Susanne Peters,
Donna and Don Hoscheit, Joe Flaherty, Cheryl Carmen, Steven Lemon,
Jeff Van Meter, Lisa Wohl, Chris Shoemaker, Kate Martiné, Gayle Kirkeby,

and of course Jerri Frantzve continue to be there with expertise, support, and involvement.

The clients I've worked with over the years deserve immeasurable tribute. I love what I do because I get to work day in and day out with brilliant, dedicated, and gifted leaders who want nothing more than to make a difference. They engage in order to continue to learn and grow. They are willing to try new, unconventional, and sometimes uncomfortable means of becoming better at their craft. They are prepared to take a hard look at themselves, and for that they are especially commended. Most importantly, they have held me and now the Lead Life Institute accountable by expecting nothing less than our best. Over the years these notable executives have continued to shape my leadership view and have informed the book's model with its behaviors and traits. Because of my educational training and background, naming clients and companies seems compromising to their anonymity. I've wrestled with this because I would not want to slight those most valued in any way. Know that discretion is my highest form of flattery. Yours are relationships that are most cherished and respected. I could not be more grateful. Special thanks also to participants of our WELL Seminars for powerful and moving leadership intensives together. Executive assistants who support our clients continue to be of great assistance to our work and are greatly appreciated for the pivotal role they play.

My perspectives are continuously and humbly informed by authors and scholars who make profound impact in their respective areas of leadership and science. Attention is called in particular to those referenced in this book. As their student I have gained greater breadth and depth.

The talented creative firm DesignSpring, Inc. tended to the book's methodical detail. Sincere gratitude is given to them for our relationship over the years and especially on this project. Kathy Bussert and Jackie Pollard are gifted artists and meticulous project managers, true right-/left-brainers. Jackie Bussert is the consummate editorial director. The right and left brain interplay was epitomized in our collaboration throughout the writing process. Thanks also to the library staff at Dutchess Community College for always being able to find the proverbial needle in the haystack, to friend and colleague Marilyn Rosskam for her editorial input, and to Gretchen Manske for her always-there administrative support. Thanks to Mark Cooper and Natalie White, extraordinary artists who continue to push me creatively.

My fondest childhood memories were of my grandparents, Swift and Lucy. My grandfather was a self-taught, self-made business success. With only a modest formal education and by faithfully reading what he referred to as his work bible, the *Wall Street Journal,* he epitomized the American dream by turning an entrepreneurial pursuit into a thriving enterprise. Fierce in his work ethic and tender at heart, his formidable character was ever apparent. My grandfather was my original inspiration for leadership. My grandmother was our quintessential source of feminine wisdom. From her I learned the power of my gender, how the feminine perspective can and will continue to drive the world's necessary evolution.

One of my fondest childhood pursuits was stargazing—not the celebrity kind, but at the stars in the sky. I sat night after night on our front lawn with my telescope marveling, wondering, and dreaming. The final acknowledgment goes to our universe, believing in its ultimate place in what we can become.

Appendix A

Worksheets

Worksheet 1 — Visioning Narrative

Write a short statement next to each heading describing how, within one year from now, you envision leading your organization's cultural development and alignment, your team's effectiveness, the performance development of key individuals, and how you as an overall leader would like to be functioning.

Cultures —

Teams —

Individuals —

Self —

Right Brain/Left Brain Leadership: Shifting Style for Maximum Impact, Mary Lou Décosterd, Praeger, 2008.

Worksheet 2 — Sponsor Feedback

Ask an individual whom you believe has a relevant perspective on your development status to complete the following (a boss, human resources person, colleague, friend, family member, or customer).

1. Comment on this leader's understanding of and alignment with the organization's culture, mission, and current goals. Note specific strengths and needs.

2. Comment on this leader's communication strengths and needs.

3. Comment on this individual's leadership style, strengths, and opportunities for development.

4. Comment on this individual's ability to influence up, down, and across the organization.

5. Comment on this individual's interpersonal skills and relationships.

6. Note any additional feedback you think would be helpful at this time.

Right Brain/Left Brain Leadership: Shifting Style for Maximum Impact, Mary Lou Décosterd, Praeger, 2008.

Worksheet 3 — Feedback Summary

Record insights and information from all current and indirect feedback sources as follows:

Formal assessment results or highlights —

Insights from any courses or seminars attended —

Performance evaluation data (note areas where you are on track versus at risk) —

Noteworthy current organizational issues, circumstances, or opportunities —

Highlights from Sponsor Feedback —

Informal feedback insights (what you are hearing or noticing that is particularly relevant) —

Right Brain/Left Brain Leadership: Shifting Style for Maximum Impact, Mary Lou Décosterd, Praeger, 2008.

Worksheet 4 — Behavior Trait Ratings

Putting together what you learned from Worksheets 1–3, for each behavior rate yourself somewhere between low and high on each trait (low is the center point of the circle). Mark the position on the chart and connect the dots. (Traits and their definitions are detailed in Chapters 3–6, if you need to review.)

Behavior Trait Ratings/Line of SITE

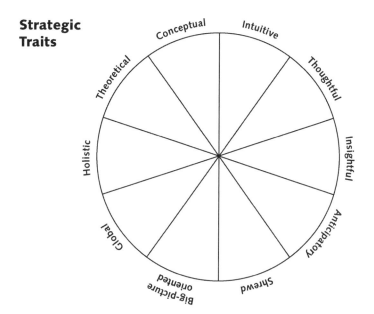

Strategic Traits

Conceptual · Intuitive · Thoughtful · Insightful · Anticipatory · Shrewd · Big-picture oriented · Global · Holistic · Theoretical

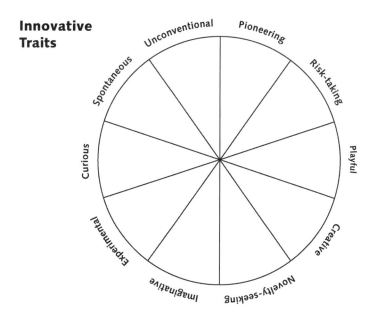

Innovative Traits

Unconventional · Pioneering · Risk-taking · Playful · Creative · Novelty-seeking · Imaginative · Experimental · Curious · Spontaneous

Right Brain/Left Brain Leadership: Shifting Style for Maximum Impact, Mary Lou Décosterd, Praeger, 2008.

Behavior Trait Ratings/Line of SITE (continued)

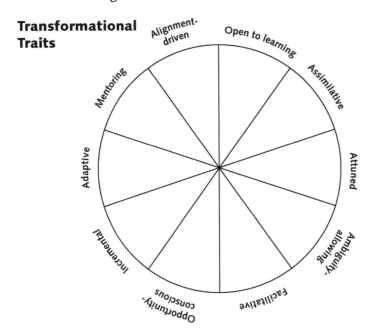

Transformational Traits

Alignment-driven · Open to learning · Assimilative · Attuned · Ambiguity-allowing · Facilitative · Opportunity-conscious · Incremental · Adaptive · Mentoring

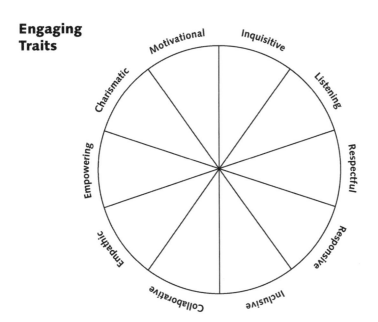

Engaging Traits

Motivational · Inquisitive · Listening · Respectful · Responsive · Inclusive · Collaborative · Empathic · Empowering · Charismatic

Right Brain/Left Brain Leadership: Shifting Style for Maximum Impact, Mary Lou Décosterd, Praeger, 2008.

Behavior Trait Ratings/MEGA Mind

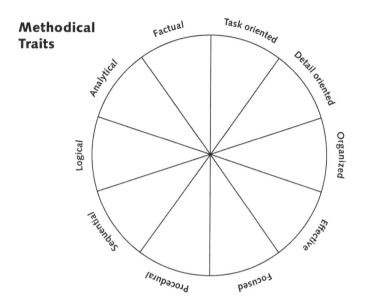

Methodical Traits

Factual · Task oriented · Detail oriented · Analytical · Organized · Logical · Effective · Sequential · Focused · Procedural

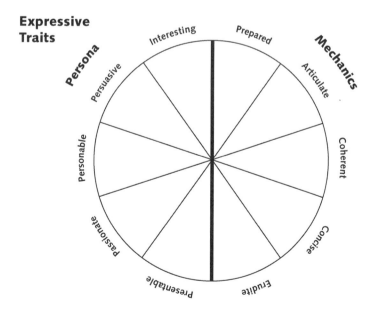

Expressive Traits

Persona · **Mechanics**

Interesting · Prepared · Persuasive · Articulate · Personable · Coherent · Passionate · Concise · Presentable · Erudite

Right Brain/Left Brain Leadership: Shifting Style for Maximum Impact, Mary Lou Décosterd, Praeger, 2008.

Behavior Trait Ratings/MEGA Mind (continued)

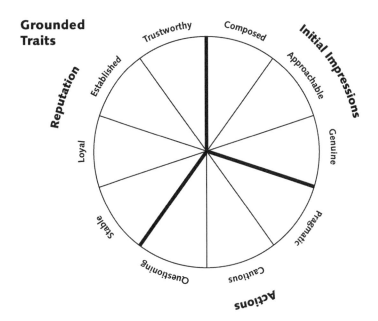

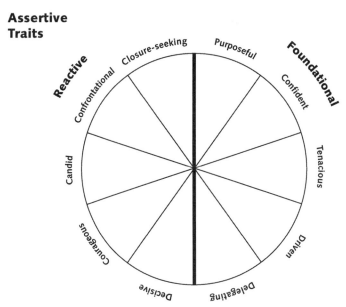

Right Brain/Left Brain Leadership: Shifting Style for Maximum Impact, Mary Lou Décosterd, Praeger, 2008.

Behavior Trait Ratings/Plus Factors

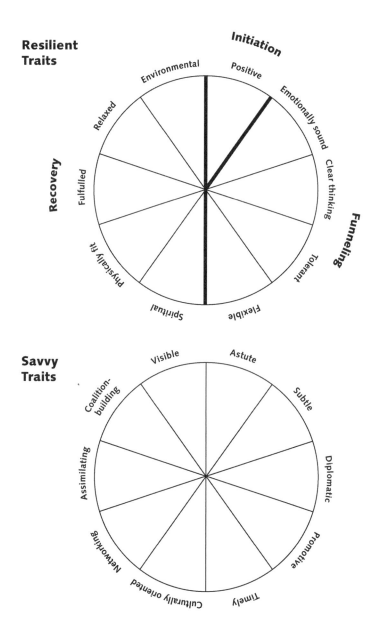

Right Brain/Left Brain Leadership: Shifting Style for Maximum Impact, Mary Lou Décosterd, Praeger, 2008.

Worksheet 5 — Visioning Summary

Use your ratings information to identify key challenges, record high and low ratings, and select 3–5 alter-brain targets.

Key Leadership Challenges: Based on your current status, feedback, and circumstance, what are your three key challenges?

1.

2.

3.

Right Brain/Left Brain Ratings: Record your high and low ratings.

Ten highest ratings:

Ten lowest ratings:

Alter-Brain Targets: Based on your current feedback and circumstance, identify the 3–5 breadth and/or depth style shifts that would most favorably impact your development. Include the specific traits that you will develop.

1.

2.

3.

4.

5.

Right Brain/Left Brain Leadership: Shifting Style for Maximum Impact, Mary Lou Décosterd, Praeger, 2008.

Worksheet 6 — Operationalizing Summary

Create a detailed plan for each of the alter-brain targets identified on Worksheet 5. Use the Tools by Trait list to help determine which tools to consider for each target. Complete a separate worksheet for each target.

Target:

Objective:

Success measure:

Time frame:

Tools:

Right Brain/Left Brain Leadership: Shifting Style for Maximum Impact, Mary Lou Décosterd, Praeger, 2008.

Worksheet 7 — Implementation Design

Describe how you will operationalize the development plan (Worksheet 6) and how you will hold yourself accountable. Complete a separate worksheet for each target.

Target:

Actions:

Accountability partners:

Date set for progress review:

Right Brain/Left Brain Leadership: Shifting Style for Maximum Impact, Mary Lou Décosterd, Praeger, 2008.

Worksheet 8 — Declaring Progress

Review your progress on developing each identified target. Reflect on your insights and determine where to go from here.

Target:

Reflections:

What have you accomplished relative to your development plan?

What tools, resources, processes worked particularly well and why?

What haven't you been able to accomplish?

Why is this so?

Course corrections and next steps:

Right Brain/Left Brain Leadership: Shifting Style for Maximum Impact, Mary Lou Décosterd, Praeger, 2008.

Tools by Trait

A suggested listing of tools that can be used for trait development

Tools Defined

These twelve tools can be used to develop any of the 100 traits in the Right Brain/Left Brain Leadership Model:

Behavior rehearsal: Practicing a new behavior until it is ingrained

Brainstorming: Generating ideas or options in a free-flowing manner

Checklists: Ordered lists to help ensure task completion

Cuing: Using an object, quote, or phrase to prompt a desired behavior

Feedback: Evaluative information from an assessment, survey, or person

Journaling: Capturing and writing about thoughts and insights

Logging: Recording factual data in a structured manner

Mentors: Experienced role models who guide and support

Mind mapping: A unique drawing process with many uses, among them to organize, plan, problem solve, broaden thinking, focus, communicate, and create

Planning aids: Technologies or systems used to structure, guide, or evaluate

Reframing: Changing a perception, in this case from a negative to a positive

Visioning: Imagining a future state through a mental picture

These tools support the development of specific traits, as noted in the list of tools by trait that follows:

Active listening: Listening attentively for meaning, implications, or empathy

Attitude setting: Moving to a desired attitude

Chaining: Taking successive steps to a desired goal

Deep breathing: Concentrated breathing activity to promote relaxation

Drawing: Creating pictures to display thoughts

Energy recovery activities: In-the-moment actions to promote energy

Extension learning: Moving from one experience to a new related one

Feedforward: Prefacing statements

Meditation: Quiet concentration attending solely on your thoughts apart from the world around you, in order to promote clarity, focus, creativity, insight, intuition, and relaxation

Questionnaires: Series of questions to gather specific information

Reflection: Considering the nature of or looking back over something

Sensory aids: Using sensory stimuli (sights, sounds, aromas, tastes, touch) to promote relaxation

Subject matter experts (SMEs): Those with depth, knowledge, and skill

Summarizing: Highlighting or recapping important aspects of something

Values clarification: A structured process to reconnect with our values

Tools by Trait

   The 100 traits are listed below along with the tools that support their development. Remember that in addition to the traits listed next to each individual trait, the following twelve tools support all traits: *behavior rehearsal, brainstorming, checklists, cuing, feedback, journaling, logging, mentors, mind mapping, planning aids, reframing, and visioning.*

The Line of SITE
Strategic

Intuitive: Active listening, reflection

Thoughtful: Active listening, deep breathing, meditation, reflection

Insightful: Active listening, drawing, meditation, reflection

Anticipatory: Active listening, chaining, reflection

Shrewd: Active listening, feedforward, reflection

Big-picture oriented: Extension learning, reflection

Global: Extension learning, reflection

Holistic: Extension learning, reflection

Theoretical: Active listening, reflection

Conceptual: Active listening, summarizing

Innovative — Extension learning supports all innovative traits

Pioneering: Chaining, energy recovery

Risk-taking: Chaining, energy recovery, reflection

Playful: Energy recovery

Creative: Chaining, reflection, sensory aids

Novelty-seeking: Chaining

Imaginative: Deep breathing, chaining, reflection, sensory aids

Experimental: Reflection

Curious: Reflection

Spontaneous: Deep breathing

Unconventional: Deep breathing, reflection

Transformational

Open to learning: Active listening, extension learning

Assimilative: Active listening, chaining, summarizing

Attuned: Active listening, reflection

Ambiguity-allowing: Active listening, deep breathing, reflection

Facilitative: Chaining, feedforward, summarizing

Opportunity-conscious: Active listening, deep breathing

Incremental: Chaining, extension learning

Adaptive: Chaining, deep breathing, reflection

Mentoring: Active listening, chaining, summarizing

Alignment-driven: Active listening, chaining, feedforward, summarizing

Engaging — Active listening supports all engaging traits

Inquisitive: Extension learning

Listening: Summarizing

Respectful: Feedforward

Responsive: Feedforward, summarizing

Inclusive: Planning aids

Collaborative: Chaining, summarizing

Empathic: Reflection, summarizing

Empowering: Chaining

Charismatic: Deep breathing, energy recovery

Motivational: Chaining, deep breathing, energy recovery, summarizing

The MEGA Mind
Methodical

Task oriented: Chaining

Detail oriented: Chaining

Organized: Chaining, summarizing

Effective: Active listening, questionnaires, summarizing

Focused: Active listening, chaining, meditation, summarizing

Procedural: Chaining, drawing

Sequential: Chaining, drawing, extension learning

Logical: Active listening, chaining, reflection, summarizing

Analytical: Active listening, chaining, questionnaires

Factual: Chaining

Expressive

Prepared: Planning aids, reflection

Articulate: Deep breathing, feedforward

Coherent: Chaining, planning aids

Concise: Summarizing

Erudite: Extension learning

Presentable: Reflection

Passionate: Chaining

Personable: Reflection, chaining

Persuasive: Reflection, active listening, feedforward

Interesting: Reflection, active listening, feedforward

Grounded

Composed: Reflection, chaining, meditation, energy recovery, feedforward

Approachable: Reflection, active listening, chaining, feedforward

Genuine: Reflection, active listening

Pragmatic: Reflection, summarizing, questionnaires, planning aids

Cautious: Reflection, active listening, chaining

Questioning: Reflection, active listening, summarizing

Stable: Reflection, chaining, meditation

Loyal: Active listening, meditation

Established: Chaining

Trustworthy: Chaining, feedforward

Assertive

Purposeful: Reflection, summarizing, planning aids

Confident: Chaining

Tenacious: Summarizing, chaining, energy recovery

Driven: Summarizing, chaining, energy recovery

Delegating: Summarizing, active listening, questionnaires, planning aids

Decisive: Summarizing, planning aids, meditation

Courageous: Chaining, energy recovery

Candid: Chaining, deep breathing

Confrontational: Summarizing, active listening, planning aids, chaining, deep breathing

Closure-seeking: Summarizing, planning aids

The Plus Factors
Resilient — Deep breathing supports all resilient traits

Positive: Chaining, energy recovery

Emotionally sound: Chaining, deep breathing, reflection, energy recovery, sensory aids, meditation

Clear thinking: Summarizing, reflection, meditation, energy recovery, sensory aids

Tolerant: Active listening, reflection, chaining, energy recovery

Flexible: Extension learning, reflection, chaining, energy recovery

Spiritual: Meditation, reflection

Physically fit: Extension learning, questionnaires, chaining, energy recovery, meditation, planning aids

Fulfilled: Values clarification, reflection, meditation

Relaxed: Chaining, sensory aids, energy recovery, meditation, sensory aids, planning aids

Environmental: Extension learning, chaining, planning aids

Savvy — Active listening supports all savvy traits

Astute: Reflection, meditation

Subtle: Reflection, deep breathing, meditation

Diplomatic: Summarizing, reflection, feedforward, meditation

Promotive: Summarizing, chaining

Timely: Reflection, meditation, deep breathing

Culturally oriented: Extension learning, chaining

Networking: Reflection, chaining, values clarification

Assimilating: Reflection, chaining, values clarification

Coalition-building: Reflection, chaining, values clarification

Visible: Reflection, chaining

APPENDIX C

LEADERSHIP LIBRARY

A suggested list for your personal leadership library, with descriptions from this author's perspective

Adams, John D. *Understanding and Managing Stress: (Vol. 2) A Book of Readings.*
   A collection of informative articles on stress and stress management techniques including, among others, meditation, the right exercise, and support networks.

Badaracco, Joseph L. *Leading Quietly: An Unorthodox Guide to Doing the Right Thing.*
   *Substantive **grounded**, **engaging**, and **savvy** resource for the empowering of what Badaracco calls "quiet leaders."*

Beckhard, Richard, and Wendy Pritchard. *Changing the Essence: The Art of Creating and Leading Fundamental Change in Organizations.*
   Accessible and complete guide to transformation and its true realities.

Benson, Herbert. *The Relaxation Response: A Simple Meditative Technique That Will Unlock Your Hidden Asset and Help You Relieve Inner Tensions, Deal More Effectively with Stress, Lower Blood Pressure, Improve Your Physical and Emotional Health.*
   Teaches a comprehensive background for the value of deep breathing and meditation in a powerful, easy-to-apply relaxation tool.

Block, Peter. *Stewardship: Choosing Service Over Self-Interest.*
   A pragmatic and innovative perspective that hallmarks a necessary evolution in leadership philosophy from top down to bottom up.

Bossidy, Larry, Ram Charan, and Charles Burck. *Execution: The Discipline of Getting Things Done.*
   A substantive and accessible guidebook for connecting the strategic to the tactical and for the cultural and people practices needed to support both.

Brandon, Rick, and Marty Seldman. *Survival of the Savvy: High-Integrity Political Tactics for Career and Company Success.*
   The resource for developing savvy along with step-by-step tools for developing your feedback and influencing skills.

Buzan, Tony. *How to Mind Map®: Make the Most of Your Mind and Learn to Create, Organize and Plan.*
   The creator of the mind map takes you through his technique in a simple, thorough manner using concise writing and great visuals.

Buzan, Tony. *Use Both Sides of Your Brain: New Mind-Mapping Techniques.*
   In-depth understanding of the workings of the right and left brain and of mind mapping's place in developing your full brain power.

Collins, Jim. *Good to Great.*
   A powerhouse work on leaders and organizations that illuminates and substantiates what it takes to get to excellence.

Connors, Roger, Tom Smith, and Craig Hickman. *The Oz Principle: Getting Results Through Individual and Organizational Accountability.*
   A powerfully engaging leadership work using a childhood classic, the story of the Wizard of Oz, and spot-on mnemonics and models to develop one's individual and organizational accountability.

Covey, Stephen R. *The 7 Habits of Highly Effective People: Powerful Lessons in Personal Change.*
   Time-honored work crucial to anyone who aspires to excellence.

Dotlich, David L., and Peter C. Cairo. *Why CEOs Fail: The 11 Behaviors That Can Derail Your Climb to the Top—And How to Manage Them.*
   The resource for understanding how self-enhancing can become self-defeating, especially when confronted with stress.

Egan, Gerard. *Working the Shadow Side: A Guide to Positive Behind-the-Scenes Management.*
   *A resource for **savvy**, for bringing what is hidden below the surface into awareness and for working that awareness in meaningful ways.*

Goleman, Daniel. *Emotional Intelligence: Why It Can Matter More Than IQ.*
   The original work regarding the groundbreaking theory of emotional intelligence, with complete related information about the brain and how to apply the theory to every aspect of our lives.

Goleman, Daniel. *Social Intelligence: The New Science of Human Relationships.*
   The original work on social intelligence theory.

Goleman, Daniel, Richard Boyatzis, and Annie McKee. *Primal Leadership: Realizing the Power of Emotional Intelligence.*
   The leadership application of emotional intelligence theory with eighteen leadership competencies for creating and sustaining optimal productivity.

Herrmann, Ned. *The Whole Brain Business Book: Unlocking the Power of Whole Brain Thinking in Organizations and Individuals.*
   Taking left and right brain thinking to the next level, Herrmann's book highlights how to get to full brain integration with emphasis on creativity and innovation as a critical determinant.

Himsel, Deborrah. *Leadership Sopranos Style: How to Become a More Effective Boss.*
   A substantive and entertaining leadership book with great concepts and lessons, including in-depth teachings on feedback.

Lencioni, Patrick M. *The Five Dysfunctions of a Team: A Leadership Fable.*
   A powerful model on team development that is accessible and simplistic, yet far-reaching in implication and impact. Includes a survey for use with your teams.

Marcum, David, Steve Smith, and Mahan Khalsa. *Business Think: Rules for Getting It Right—Now, and No Matter What.*
   A breakthrough work on the necessary mindset and actions of a truly strategic leader, with behavioral imperatives.

Maxwell, John C. *Attitude 101: What Every Leader Needs to Know.*
   A profound collection of insights on leadership, attitude, and impact. Compact, easy to read over and over again. A wonderful resource for cues and inspirations.

Patterson, Kerry, Joseph Grenny, Ron McMillan, and Al Switzler. *Crucial Conversations: Tools for Talking When Stakes Are High.*
   Substantive resource for communicating with impact.

Reiman, Tonya. *The Power of Body Language: How to Succeed in Every Business and Social Encounter.*
   A thorough, practical, and insightful guide to understanding and leveraging nonverbal cues.

Roizen, Michael F., and Mehmet Oz. *You: The Owner's Manual: An Insider's Guide to the Body That Will Make You Healthier and Younger.*
   A comprehensive and engaging all-around health resource from the quintessential experts.

Slywotzky, Adrian. *The Art of Profitability.*
   Twenty-three must-know lessons to inform business strategy, taught through the lens of a delightfully provocative, Zen-like master.

Stone, Douglas, Bruce Patton, and Sheila Heen. *Difficult Conversations: How to Discuss What Matters Most.*
   Substantive resource for negotiating complex communication obstacles.

Varney, Glenn H. *Building Productive Teams: An Action Guide and Resource Book.*
   A tool-packed, accessible guidebook for developing teams.

Zander, Rosamund S., and Benjamin Zander. *The Art of Possibility: Transforming Professional and Personal Life.*
   An engaging work by two model collaborators on how to take innovative thinking to the next level.

NOTES

Chapter 1

1. *Random House College Dictionary*, 1975, s.v. "leader" and "leadership."
2. Broader definition of leadership derived from our work with clients at the Lead Life Institute.
3. Carlson, *Physiology of Behavior*, 88–95; and Garrett, *Brain and Behavior*, 60–62.
4. Carlson, *Physiology of Behavior*, 11–12; and Garrett, *Brain and Behavior*, 61–68.
5. John L. Bradshaw and Lesley J. Rogers, "Evolution of Lateral Asymmetries, Language, Tool Use, and Intellect," *Canadian Journal of Experimental Psychology* (Ottawa) 47, no. 4 (1993): 757; Buzan, *Use Both Sides of Your Brain*, 17–18; Lesley S.J. Farmer, "Left Brain, Right Brain, Whole Brain," *School Library Media Activities Monthly* 21, no. 2 (2004): 27–28; Gazzaniga, "Split Brain Revisited," John Rennie, ed., "The Hidden Mind," *Scientific American* (December 2002): 26–31; Jerre Levy, "Possible Basis for the Evolution of Lateral Specialization of the Human Brain," *Nature* 224, no. 5219 (1969): 614–615; Rachel Nowak, "Nerve Cells Mirror Brain's Left-Right Divide," *New Scientist* 178, no. 2395 (2003): 20; Sousa, *How the Brain Learns*, 170–178, 191–193; Sperry, "Brain Bisection and Consciousness," in Eccles, ed., *Brain and Conscious Experience*, 298–314; and Springer and Deutsch, *Left Brain, Right Brain* 12–19.
6. Buzan, *Use Both Sides of Your Brain*, 17–18.
7. Garrett, *Brain and Behavior*, 73.
8. Buzan, *Use Both Sides of Your Brain*, 9.
9. Roizen and Oz, *Owner's Manual* 87–90.
10. Dudley Lynch, "Is the Brain Stuff Still the Right (or Left) Stuff?" *Training and Development Journal* (Madison) 40, no. 2 (1986): 22–26.
11. Gazzaniga, "Split Brain Revisited," Rennie, "The Hidden Mind," 26–31.
12. Carlson, *Physiology of Behavior*, 100–102; and Garrett, *Brain and Behavior*, 75–78.

13. Carlson, *Physiology of Behavior,* 102–103.

14. Garrett, *Brain and Behavior,* 201.

15. T.B. Herbert, et al., "Cardiovascular Reactivity and the Course of Immune Response to an Acute Psychological Stressor," *Psychosomatic Medicine* 56, no. 4 (1994): 337–344.

16. Adams, *Understanding and Managing Stress,* 1–2, 10.

17. Antonio R. Damasio, et al., "Subcortical and Cortical Brain Activity During the Feeling of Self-Generated Emotions," *Nature Neuroscience* 3, no. 10 (2000): 1049–1056.

18. Garrett, *Brain and Behavior,* 199.

19. Carlson, *Physiology of Behavior,* 91; Paul D. MacLean, "Psychosomatic Disease and the 'Visceral Brain': Recent Developments Bearing on the Papez Theory of Emotion," *Psychosomatic Medicine* 11 (1949): 338–353; and James W. Papez, "A Proposed Mechanism of Emotion," *Archives of Neurology and Psychiatry* 38 (1937): 725–743.

20. Goleman, *Emotional Intelligence: Why It Can Matter More than IQ,* 9–19.

21. Darwin, *Expression of Emotions in Man and Animals,* 40–41, 176–179.

22. Tavris, *Misunderstood Emotion,* 17–47.

23. Goleman, *Social Intelligence,* 4.

Chapter 2

1. The development of the Right Brain / Left Brain Leadership Model, its behaviors, and corresponding traits, represents a synthesis of my experiences as an educator, clinician, organizational consultant, and business executive. Believing in the power of defined behaviors to guide leadership and in the inherent complexity of those behaviors, the model was created to illuminate nuances and to be as all-inclusive as possible. The development of the right brain / left brain leadership behaviors and corresponding traits was informed by my university teaching and ongoing work practice, and by the following sources: Badaracco, *Leading Quietly;* Beckhard and Pritchard, *Changing the Essence;* Block, *Stewardship;* Bossidy, Charan, and Burck, *Execution;* Brandon and Seldman, *Survival of the Savvy;* Collins, *Good to Great;* Connors, Smith, and Hickman, *Oz Principle;* Egan, *Working the Shadow Side;* Goleman, Boyatzis, and McKee, *Primal Leadership;* Himsel, *Leadership Sopranos Style;* Marcum, Smith, and Khalsa, *Business Think;* Maxwell, *Attitude 101;* Patterson, et al., *Crucial Conversations;* Slater, *Leadership Secrets from Jack Welch;* and Stone, Patton, and Heen, *Difficult Conversations.*

2. Chapter 2 not only presents the model's behaviors and their corresponding traits, but it also calls attention to the leader's role with respect to culture and team development. Attention to culture and teams was informed by my university education and teaching, by my ongoing work practice, and by the following sources: Beer, *Organizational Change and Development;* Goleman, Boyatzis, and McKee, *Primal Leadership;* Homans, *Social Behavior;* Lencioni, *Five Dysfunctions of a Team;* Lippitt, *Organizational Renewal;* Reed and Hughes, *Rethinking Organization;* Schein, "Organizational Culture," *American Psychologist* 45 (1990); Varney, *Building Productive Teams;* and Welch and Byrne, *Jack: Straight from the Gut.*

3. Bossidy, Charan, and Burck, *Execution,* 92.

Chapter 3

1. *Wikipedia: The Free Encyclopedia*, s.v. "Howard Schultz," http://en.wikipedia.org/wiki/Howard_Schultz (accessed August 29, 2007).
2. Quotation from *Brainy Quote*, George Burns, http://www.brainyquote.com/quotes.author.g.george_burns.html (accessed September 1, 2007).
3. Quotation from *SelfGrowth.com*, Giten on Intuition and Healing, http://www.selfgrowth.com/articles/GITEN2.html (accessed September 14, 2007).
4. Krebs Hirsh and Kummerow, *Introduction to Type® in Organizations*, 1–4.
5. *Wikipedia: The Free Encyclopedia*, s.v. "tai chi chuan," http://en.wikipedia.org/wiki/Tai_chi (accessed June 7, 2007).
6. Buzan, *How to Mind Map®*, 12, 22–31.
7. Zander and Zander, *The Art of Possibility*, 14.
8. Quotation from *The Quotations Page*, Stephen Nachmanovitch, http://www.quotationspage.com/quote/27091html (accessed July 2, 2007).
9. Moustakas, *Phenomenological Research Methods*, 58–60.
10. Sharf, *Theories of Psychotherapy and Counseling*, 250–288; Goleman, Boyatzis, and McKee, *Primal Leadership*, 35–52. References to the value of awareness are supported by the principles of Gestalt psychology and by Goleman's emotional intelligence leadership competencies.
11. Felder, *100 Most Influential Women of All Time*, 60–62.
12. Alexander, *Fifty Black Women Who Changed America*, 108–114.
13. Parsons, *Skilled Consultant*, 71–102; Eagly and Chaiken, *Psychology of Attitudes*, 568–589.
14. Beckhard and Pritchard, *Changing the Essence*, 81.
15. Quotation from *The Quotations Page*, Douglas MacArthur, http://www.quotationspage.com/quote/1954html (accessed August 17, 2007).
16. Sharf, *Theories of Psychotherapy and Counseling*, 292–332, 375–416. References to progressive steps to behavior change and to cuing are supported by the principles of behavioral and cognitive-behavioral psychology.
17. Beckhard and Pritchard, *Changing the Essence*, 77–80.
18. Ibid., 9–24.
19. Egan, *Working the Shadow Side*, 138–144.
20. Sharf, *Theories of Psychotherapy and Counseling*, 215–246. References to empathy are supported by the principles of humanistic psychology, in particular, client-centered approaches.
21. DeVito, *Interpersonal Communications Book*, 241.

Chapter 4

1. Buzan, *How to Mind Map®*, 12.
2. Alexander, *Fifty Black Women Who Changed America*, 208.
3. Benson, *Relaxation Response*, 78–79.
4. Roizen and Oz, *Owner's Manual*, 151, 166.
5. MacDonald and Schoenberger, "100 Most Powerful Women," *Forbes*, July 27, 2005, http://www.forbes.com/2005/07/27/powerful-women-world-cz_05powom_land.html (accessed August 30, 2007); *Wikipedia: The Free Encyclopedia*,

s.v. "Wu Yi," http://en.wikipedia.org/wiki/Wu_Yi (accessed November 20, 2007).

6. Dotlich and Cairo, *Why CEOs Fail*, 1–12, 27–38; Hogan and Hogan, "Assessing Leadership," *International Journal of Selection and Assessment* 9, no. 1–2 (2001): 40–51.

Chapter 5

1. Susanne Décosterd, physical therapist, personal conversation with author, July 5, 2005.
2. Maxwell, *Attitude 101*, 1, 13–14.
3. Carlson, *Physiology of Behavior*, 260, 271; Roizen and Oz, *Owner's Manual*, 160.
4. Goleman, "Meditation Helps Break the Stress Cycle," in Adams, *Understanding and Managing Stress*, 147–153; Cooksley, *Healing Home Spa*, 36.
5. Jessica Tonna, wellness practitioner, personal conversation with author, September 9, 2006; Shari Simon, wellness practitioner, personal conversation with author, October 12, 2006.
6. Holli Beckwith, wellness practitioner, personal conversation with author, September 6, 2006.

Chapter 6

1. Serafin, "The World's Most Powerful Women in Politics," *Forbes*, August 30, 2007, http://www.forbes.com/2007/08/30/power-women-politicians-07women-cz_ts_0830politics.html (accessed August 31, 2007).
2. Quotation from *The Quotations Page*, Aristotle, http://www.quotationspage.com/quote/24240.html (accessed July 21, 2007).
3. Brandon and Seldman, *Survival of the Savvy*, 2.
4. Ibid., 24–53.
5. Badaracco, *Leading Quietly*, 1–10.
6. DeVito, *Interpersonal Communications Book*, 360–363.
7. Ibid., 71–74.
8. Sharf, *Theories of Psychotherapy and Counseling*, 250.
9. Goleman, *Social Intelligence*, 43.
10. Himsel, *Leadership Sopranos Style*, 89.
11. DeVito, *Interpersonal Communications Book*, 15–16.

Chapter 7

1. Dvorak and Badal, "This Is Your Brain on the Job," *Wall Street Journal*, September 20, 2007.

BIBLIOGRAPHY

Adams, John D., ed. *Understanding and Managing Stress: (Vol. 2) A Book of Readings.* San Diego: University Associates, 1980.

Alexander, Amy. *Fifty Black Women Who Changed America.* New York: Citadel Press, 1999.

Altman, Irwin, and Dalmas Taylor. *Social Penetration: The Development of Interpersonal Relationships.* New York: Holt, Rinehart and Winston, 1973.

Badaracco, Joseph L. *Leading Quietly: An Unorthodox Guide to Doing the Right Thing.* Boston: Harvard Business School Press, 2002.

Barker, L.I., K.L. Wahlers, and K.M. Watson. *Groups in Process: An Introduction to Small Group Communication.* 5th ed. Boston: Allyn and Bacon, 1995.

Beckhard, Richard, and Wendy Pritchard. *Changing the Essence: The Art of Creating and Leading Fundamental Change in Organizations.* San Francisco: Jossey-Bass, 1992.

Beer, Michael. *Organizational Change and Development: A Systems View.* Santa Monica: Goodyear, 1980.

Benson, Herbert. *The Relaxation Response: A Simple Meditative Technique That Will Unlock Your Hidden Asset and Help You Relieve Inner Tensions, Deal More Effectively with Stress, Lower Blood Pressure, Improve Your Physical and Emotional Health.* New York: William Morrow, 1975.

Blau, Peter. *Exchange and Power in Social Life.* New York: Wiley, 1964.

Block, Peter. *Stewardship: Choosing Service Over Self-Interest.* San Francisco: Berrett-Koehler, 1993.

Bossidy, Larry, Ram Charan, and Charles Burck. *Execution: The Discipline of Getting Things Done.* New York: Crown Business, 2002.

Bradshaw, John L., and Lesley J. Rogers. "The Evolution of Lateral Asymmetries, Language, Tool Use, and Intellect." *Canadian Journal of Experimental Psychology* (Ottawa, Canada) 47, no. 4 (1993): 757.

Brandon, Rick, and Marty Seldman. *Survival of the Savvy: High-Integrity Political Tactics for Career and Company Success.* New York: Free Press, 2004.

Brehm, Sharon S., and Saul M. Kassin. *Social Psychology.* 3rd ed. Boston: Houghton Mifflin, 1996.

Brown, Marvin R., George F. Koob, and Catherine Rivier, eds. *Stress: Neurobiology and Neuroendocrinology.* New York: Dekker, 1990.

Buzan, Tony. *How to Mind Map®: Make the Most of Your Mind and Learn to Create, Organize and Plan.* London: Thorsons, 2003.

Buzan, Tony. *Use Both Sides of Your Brain: New Mind-Mapping Techniques.* 3rd ed. New York: Plume, 1991.

Carlson, Neil R. *Physiology of Behavior.* 5th ed. Needham Heights, MA: Allyn and Bacon, 1994.

Collins, Jim. *Good to Great.* New York: HarperBusiness, 2001.

Connors, Roger, Tom Smith, and Craig Hickman. *The Oz Principle: Getting Results Through Individual and Organizational Accountability.* New York: Portfolio Hardcover, 2004.

Cooksley, Valerie Gennari. *Healing Home Spa: Soothe Your Symptoms, Ease Your Pain and Age-proof Your Body with Pleasure Remedies.* New York: Prentice Hall Press, 2003.

Covey, Stephen R. *The 7 Habits of Highly Effective People: Powerful Lessons in Personal Change.* New York: Fireside, 1990.

Damasio, Antonio R., T.J. Grabowski, A. Bechara, H. Damasio, L.L. Ponto, J. Parvizi, and R.D. Hichwa. "Subcortical and Cortical Brain Activity During the Feeling of Self-Generated Emotions." *Nature Neuroscience* 3, no. 10 (2000): 1049–1056.

Darwin, Charles. *The Expression of the Emotions in Man and Animals.* New York: Philosophical Library, 1955. Original work published in 1872.

DeVito, Joseph A. *The Interpersonal Communications Book.* 8th ed. New York: Longman, 1998.

Dotlich, David L., and Peter C. Cairo. *Why CEOs Fail: The 11 Behaviors That Can Derail Your Climb to the Top—And How to Manage Them.* San Francisco: Jossey-Bass, 2003.

Dvorak, Phred, and Jaclyne Badal. "This Is Your Brain on the Job: Neuroscientists Are Finding That Business Leaders Really May Think Differently." *Wall Street Journal,* September 20, 2007.

Eagly, Alice H., and Shelly Chaiken. *The Psychology of Attitudes.* Fort Worth, TX: Harcourt Brace Jovanovich College Publishers, 1993.

Eccles, J.C., ed. *Brain and Conscious Experience.* New York: Springer-Verlag, 1966.

Egan, Gerard. *Working the Shadow Side: A Guide to Positive Behind-the-Scenes Management.* San Francisco: Jossey-Bass, 1994.

Farmer, Lesley S.J. "Left Brain, Right Brain, Whole Brain." *School Library Media Activities Monthly* 21, no. 2 (2004): 27–28.

Felder, Deborah G. *The 100 Most Influential Women of All Time.* New York: Citadel Press, 2001. Updated and revised.

Forsyth, Donelson R. *Group Dynamics.* 2nd ed. Pacific Grove, CA: Brooks/Cole, 1990.

Garrett, Bob. *Brain and Behavior.* Belmont, CA: Wadsworth, 2003.

Goleman, Daniel. *Emotional Intelligence: Why It Can Matter More Than IQ.* New York: Bantam Books, 1995.

Goleman, Daniel. *Social Intelligence: The New Science of Human Relationships.* New York: Bantam Books, 2006.

Goleman, Daniel, Richard Boyatzis, and Annie McKee. *Primal Leadership: Realizing the Power of Emotional Intelligence.* Boston: Harvard Business School Press, 2002.

Herbert, T.B., S. Cohen, A.L. Marsland, E.A. Bachen, B.S. Rabin, M.F. Muldoon, and S.B. Manuck. "Cardiovascular Reactivity and the Course of Immune Response to an Acute Psychological Stressor." *Psychosomatic Medicine* 56, no. 4 (1994): 337–344.

Herrmann, Ned. *The Whole Brain Business Book: Unlocking the Power of Whole Brain Thinking in Organizations and Individuals.* New York: McGraw-Hill, 1996.

Himsel, Deborrah. *Leadership Sopranos Style: How to Become a More Effective Boss.* Chicago: Dearborn, 2003.

Hogan, Robert, and Joyce Hogan. "Assessing Leadership: A View from the Dark Side." *International Journal of Selection and Assessment* 9 (2001): 40–51.

Homans, George C. *Social Behavior: Its Elementary Forms.* New York: Harcourt Brace Jovanovich, 1961.

Johnson, David W., and Frank P. Johnson. *Joining Together: Group Theory and Group Skills.* 5th ed. Boston: Allyn and Bacon, 1994.

Krebs Hirsh, Sandra, and Jean M. Kummerow. *Introduction to Type® in Organizations.* 3rd ed. Mountain View, CA: CPP, Inc., 1998.

LeDoux, Joseph E. "Emotional Memory Systems in the Brain." *Behavioural Brain Research* 58, no. 12 (1993): 69–79.

Lencioni, Patrick M. *The Five Dysfunctions of a Team: A Leadership Fable.* San Francisco: Jossey-Bass, 2002.

Levenson, Robert W., Paul Ekman, and Wallace V. Friesen. "Voluntary Facial Action Generates Emotion-Specific Autonomic Nervous System Activity." *Psychophysiology* 27, no. 4 (1990): 363–384.

Levy, Jerre. "Possible Basis for the Evolution of Lateral Specialization of the Human Brain." *Nature* 224, no. 5219 (1969): 614–615.

Lippitt, George L. *Organizational Renewal: A Holistic Approach to Organization Development.* 2nd ed. Englewood Cliffs, NJ: Prentice Hall, 1982.

Lynch, Dudley. "Is the Brain Stuff Still the Right (or Left) Stuff?" *Training and Development Journal* (Madison) 40, no. 2 (1986): 22–26.

MacDonald, Elizabeth, and Chana R. Schoenberger. "The 100 Most Powerful Women." Special report. *Forbes*, July 28, 2005. http://www.forbes.com/2005/07/27/powerful-women-world-cz_05powom_land.html (accessed August 30, 2007).

MacLean, Paul D. "Psychosomatic Disease and the 'Visceral Brain': Recent Developments Bearing on the Papez Theory of Emotion." *Psychosomatic Medicine* 11 (1949): 338–353.

Marcum, David, Steve Smith, and Mahan Khalsa. *Business Think: Rules for Getting It Right—Now, and No Matter What!* New York: Wiley, 2002.

Matousek, Mark. "We're Wired to Connect." *AARP: The Magazine,* January–February 2007, 36–38.

Maxwell, John C. *Attitude 101: What Every Leader Needs to Know.* Nashville: Thomas Nelson, 2003.

Moustakas, Clark. *Phenomenological Research Methods.* Thousand Oaks, CA: Sage, 1994.

Myers, Isabelle Briggs. *Introduction to Type®.* 6th ed. Mountain View, CA: CPP, Inc., 1998.

Nowak, Rachel. "Nerve Cells Mirror Brain's Left-Right Divide." *New Scientist* 178, no. 2395 (2003): 20.

Papez, James W. "A Proposed Mechanism of Emotion." *Archives of Neurology and Psychiatry* 38 (1937): 725–743.

Parsons, Richard P. *The Skilled Consultant: A Systematic Approach to the Theory and Practice of Consultation.* Needham Heights, MA: Allyn and Bacon, 1996.

Patterson, Kerry, Joseph Grenny, Ron McMillan, and Al Switzler. *Crucial Conversations: Tools for Talking When Stakes Are High.* New York: McGraw-Hill, 2002.

Reed, Michael, and Michael Hughes. *Rethinking Organization: New Directions in Organization Theory and Analysis.* London: Sage, 1992.

Reiman, Tonya. *The Power of Body Language: How to Succeed in Every Business and Social Environment.* New York: Pocket Books, 2007.

Rennie, John, ed. "The Hidden Mind." Special issue. *Scientific American,* December 2002, 26–31.

Roizen, Michael F., and Mehmet Oz. *You: The Owner's Manual: An Insider's Guide to the Body That Will Make You Healthier and Younger.* New York: HarperCollins, 2005.

Russell, Ronald, ed. *Focusing the Whole Brain: Transforming Your Life with Hemispheric Synchronization.* Charlottesville, VA: Hampton Roads, 2004.

Schein, Edgar H. "Organizational Culture." *American Psychologist* 45 (1990): 109–119.

Schnell, Eugene R., and Allen L. Hammel. *Introduction to the FIRO-B Instrument in Organizations.* Mountain View, CA: CPP, Inc., 1993.

Schutz, Will. *FIRO: A Three Dimensional Theory of Interpersonal Behavior.* 3rd ed. New York: Holt, Rinehart and Winston, 1998.

Serafin, Tatiana. "The World's Most Powerful Women in Politics." *Forbes,* August 30, 2007. http://www.forbes.com/2007/08/30/power-women-politicians-07women-cz_ts_0830politics.html (accessed August 31, 2007).

Sharf, Richard S. *Theories of Psychotherapy and Counseling: Concepts and Cases.* Pacific Grove, CA: Brooks/Cole, 1996.

Slater, Robert. *29 Leadership Secrets from Jack Welch.* New York: McGraw-Hill, 2002.

Slywotzky, Adrian. *The Art of Profitability.* New York: Warner Books, 2002.

Sousa, David A. *How the Brain Learns.* 2nd ed. Thousand Oaks, CA: Corwin Press, 2000.

Springer, Sally P., and Georg Deutsch. *Left Brain, Right Brain: Perspectives from Cognitive Neuroscience.* 5th ed. New York: W.H. Freeman, 1998.

Stone, Douglas, Bruce Patton, and Sheila Heen. *Difficult Conversations: How to Discuss What Matters Most.* New York: Penguin, 2000.

Tavris, Carol. *Anger: The Misunderstood Emotion.* New York: Simon and Schuster, 1983.

Varney, Glenn H. *Building Productive Teams: An Action Guide and Resource Book.* San Francisco: Jossey-Bass, 1989.

Wagner, Helmut R. *Phenomenology of Consciousness and Sociology of the Life-World: An Introductory Study.* Edmonton, Canada: University of Alberta Press, 1983.

Welch, Jack, and John A. Byrne. *Jack: Straight from the Gut.* New York: Warner Books, 2001.

Zander, Rosamund S., and Benjamin Zander. *The Art of Possibility: Transforming Professional and Personal Life.* Boston: Harvard Business School Press, 2000.

INDEX

About the Author and the Lead Life Institute

MARY LOU DÉCOSTERD, PHD is founder and managing executive of the Lead Life Institute, a learning consultancy offering programs and services to help executives, teams, and organizations become their best. Dr. Décosterd has twenty-five years of experience in organizational development, applied psychology, and university teaching. She also has authored a children's book series titled The Adventures of Magical Max.

Dr. Décosterd is adept at assessing individual and organizational needs and obtaining results. She works as an executive coach to leaders and leadership teams and as a facilitator, speaker, designer, and trainer for both profit and nonprofit organizations. Areas of expertise include leadership and interpersonal development, implementation and execution, cultural and team alignment, strategic change leadership, mediation, attitude and motivation, wellness, and work/life integration. Her work focuses around four critical success drivers: business acumen, influencing, executing, and self-satisfaction.

Prior to founding the Lead Life Institute, Dr. Décosterd was a partner at Executive Partners, a Chicago-headquartered international consulting firm, and before working for Executive Partners she had her own consulting practice, was a tenured university professor, and held high-level leadership positions in the nonprofit sector.

Dr. Décosterd has lived and worked in the United States and abroad. She is a graduate of the University of Hartford, the University of Oklahoma, and the Fielding Institute. She holds a BA in psychology; master's degrees in educational psychology, organizational development, and clinical psychology;

post-master's certification in community psychology; and a PhD in human development. She has been recognized by "Who's Who in Teaching" and "Outstanding Women of America."

THE LEAD LIFE INSTITUTE is a research-based learning consultancy offering dynamic programs and services to help executives and their teams realize their potential and become their best. Recognizing the challenges, opportunities, and complexities of today's world, the Lead Life Institute provides state-of-the-art approaches for business and organizational success. As the name indicates, the Lead Life Institute focuses on the successful integration of leadership and life skills. "Leadership" is a broad term encompassing business and professional acumen, how the leader favorably impacts the world, and how the leader makes a difference. The "life" aspect focuses on attitude, interpersonal power, and resilience. The overall aim of the Lead Life Institute is to help individuals and organizations attain next-level success through sound strategic leadership and strong, aligned operating cultures.

The Lead Life Institute offers executive coaching, leadership development, women's executive development, team excellence, and training design and delivery in more than twenty areas of expertise, as well as work/life success seminars and individual/organizational assessments.

THE LEAD LIFE
INSTITUTE, LLC
Helping you to be your best

www.leadlifeinstitute.com